FAMILY

in the

NORTH WALES BORDERLANDS

Gordon Emery

Scarthin Books, Cromford, Derbyshire 1992

FAMILY WALKS
in the
NORTH WALES BORDERLANDS

Family Walks Series
General Editor: Norman Taylor

THE COUNTRY CODE

Guard against all risk of fire
Fasten all gates
Keep dogs under proper control
Keep to paths across farmland
Avoid damaging fences, hedges and walls
Leave no litter
Safeguard water supplies
Protect wildlife,wild plants and trees
Go carefully along country roads
Respect the life of the countryside

Published by Scarthin Books, Cromford, Derbyshire

Phototypesetting, printing by Nuffield Press Ltd., Cowley, Oxford.

ISBN 0 907758 50 9

VALLE CRUCIS ABBEY, NEAR LLANGOLLEN

Acknowledgements

To Jim Bentley and Clwyd Record Office for details of the tramway in Glyndyfrdwy

Tony Bowerman for advice.

Dragon Snaps, Llangollen, who printed the photographs.

About the author

Gordon Emery was born in Ulverston, on the southwestern edge of the English Lakes. After being educated in North London he worked as an apprentice printer, trainee glass-blower, solicitor's clerk, roadsweeper, builder's labourer, walk leader, barman, security guard, supervisor of a countryside 'Taskforce' team working for the Lake District Planning Board, storeman, motorbike and car stunt show organiser, and has restored a Welsh cottage.

He became a walks' writer when he helped produce 15 'Walks Around Wrexham Maelor' for Clwyd County Council and went on to write some 26 more local guides and to become his own publisher with 'Walks in Clwyd'. He has recently produced the 'Guide to the Maelor Way' and co-authored a Daywalks guide to the 'Vale of Llangollen'.

Gordon is a Ramblers' Association Footpath Inspector and has voluntarily installed over 190 stiles and bridges in Clwyd. Since then he has erected another 200 in his work for Wrexham Maelor Borough Council.

He lives in Chester with his wife, who is a teacher of Alexander Technique and violin, and his two sons.

CONTENTS

LOCATION MAP

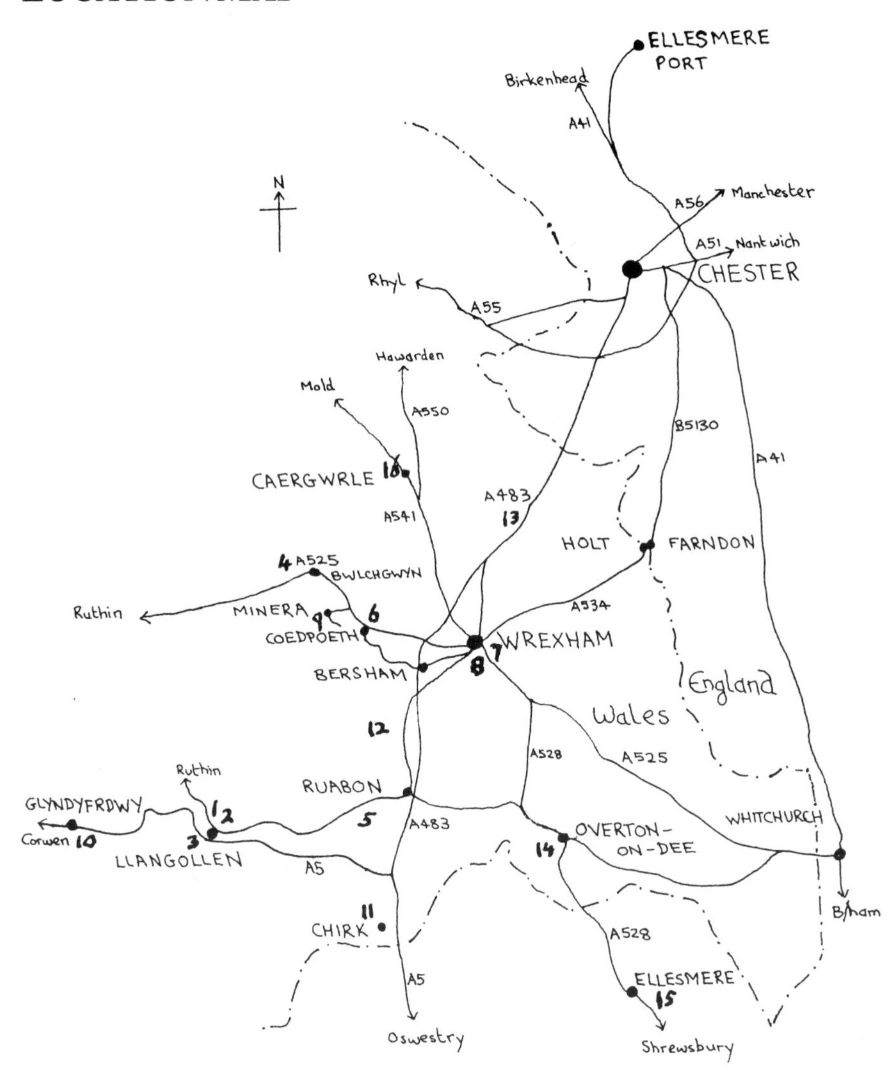

Introduction

When I told my eldest son that I was writing a book in the 'Family Walks' series, he soon brought me down to earth. Whereas I had chosen several walks for their historical or archaeological interest, he insisted on routes with water, caves or viewpoints. Since then, I have designed these 16 walks, and my family and I have tested them. A few are shorter versions of my Clwyd guides rewritten and walked with my youngest son, aged 4. There are interesting caves near two of the routes, but though there are clear paths to them, these paths are not 'legal' rights-of-way.

The borderlands are often used only as a stopping off point for Snowdonia and the North Wales coast, but to travel miles by car to these areas for a short walk is environmentally unsound. In contrast, there are many fascinating walks closer to home, in the Borderlands. After five years exploring Wrexham and the surrounding area I have still only used perhaps half the public paths and there are many that I would revisit time and time again.

There is a wealth of flora here: I know one spot where I can stand and see five varieties of orchid from a public path and another where I have found five varieties of edible fungi. In autumn the lanes, unlike those in many English counties nowadays, are so full of blackberries it is hardly worth taking a picnic. In winter the footprints of a variety of wildlife recreate the drama of last night's hunt or show the morning's play.

Public transport & timing

All these walks can be reached by public transport—so why not leave your car, your cares and your pollution at home? Children love travelling by bus and train, even if they are used to going by car. It may not be as quick, but you can make a day's outing by having a meal or picnic as well. Take your time on the walks, especially with young children. For children under 8 allow at least an hour for every mile. Don't worry if you get a few 'How far is it now?' comments. Counter them with 'Are you going to be the leader?' or 'What is that ahead?' and soon you'll be getting 'Can we go to Nant Mill?' or 'Can we go to that castle again?'

Remember to check return times before you start.

Food and drink

Many of the routes have cafés or other refreshment stops nearby but it is always a good idea to take a snack and drinks, and fun to take a picnic anyway. Hot food can be carried in a wide-necked Thermos flask or its plastic equivalent for safety. When I used to work on paths in the Lake District fells during winter I took a litre flask of curried chick peas and vegetables, or similar. I often ended up sharing my food with co-workers who had eaten their sandwiches and were enviously watching my steaming bowl.

What to wear

As long as your child's shoes are comfortable and have good grips on the soles almost any footwear is suitable. (I walked all the routes in sandals.) Do not go out and buy a pair of heavy walking boots which will need 'wearing-in' anyway and may put your children off walking for life. On the other hand some children love wearing special walking equipment and will walk with more enthusiasm, especially with some of the lightweight boots on the market today. If a pair of trainers is likely to get soaked after wet weather, take a spare pair and some dry socks to change into when the walk is completed.

It pays to be prepared. Always carry lightweight rainwear if there is a sign of a cloud, and in winter ensure that you have extra clothing.

Wet weather days

It is fun to walk in the rain but miserable if you get too wet. Choose a short route with shelter nearby. Lists of visitors' centres, museums, swimming pools and other useful telephone numbers are given in the appendices at the back of the book.

BLACKTHORN white blossom, sloes in autumn

Choosing a walk

If you are not sure of the area or how far your children will walk, choose one from the top of the list in the appendices at the back of the book. Most of the longer routes include a short cut, and if you are less than halfway around you can always turn back. On one walk my youngest son did 4 miles one day from Nant Mill and then, a week later when checking the directions, took two hours to go less than half a mile and preferred spending his time down by the stream and on the play equipment.

Rights of way

As soon as you leave the public right-of-way you fail to be insured by the County Council and are probably on private land. If fields are ploughed or crops growing you should walk single file in the right direction. If, on public rights-of-way, you meet an obstruction you can, by law, take the nearest route around.

Some of the routes that I wanted to include in this book were too difficult, due to illegal obstructions. A recent survey showed that 80% of circular walks in Wales could not be completed because of this type of problem—perhaps one reason why people buy walk guides. At the time of writing, all these 16 routes were free of major obstructions and crops, although there were some stiles in need of repair.

If you walk on any public footpaths in the area and find difficulties, please write to the County Council (see the appendices for addresses). The Council do not check rights of way themselves and only look into problems when they are reported by members of the public.

Maps

No extra maps are needed for these walks but is worth buying them for any district you walk in regularly. The Ordnance Survey 1 : 25000 Pathfinder maps show paths and field boundaries. Two of them—Wrexham North, and Wrexham South & Llangollen—cover most of these walks and the majority of Wrexham Maelor. Here the footpaths are under a programme of revitalisation: the Communities of Minera, Penycae, Holt, Hanmer, Rhos and Overton are virtually free of obstructions now although a few bridges are still awaited. For a list of maps covering the Borderlands see the appendices.

Symbols used on the route maps

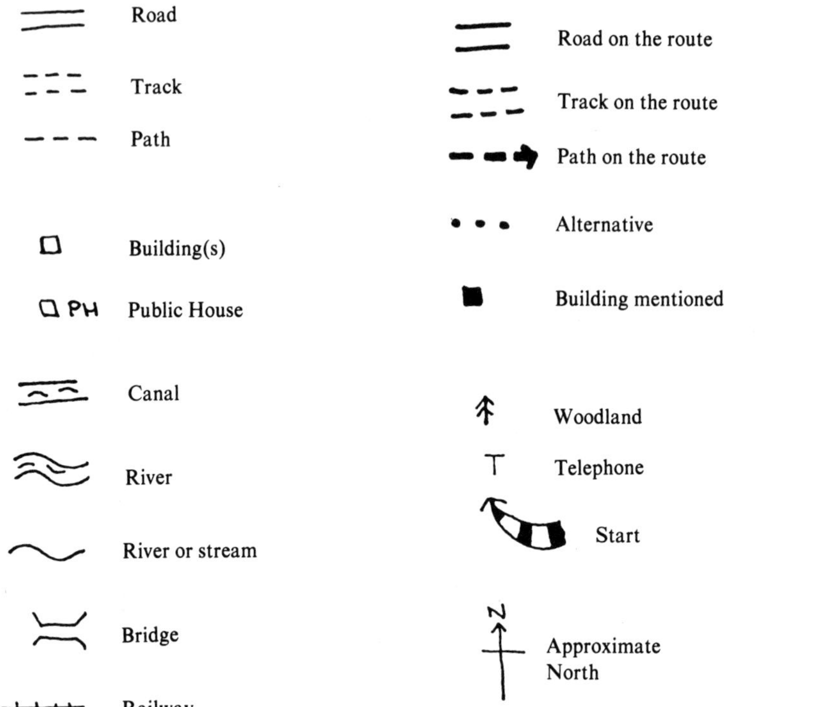

Road

Track

Path

Building(s)

PH Public House

Canal

River

River or stream

Bridge

Railway

Road on the route

Track on the route

Path on the route

Alternative

Building mentioned

Woodland

Telephone

Start

N

Approximate North

NONE OF THE MAPS ARE TO SCALE

Numbers denote route directions

Route 1 **1¾ or 4 miles**

Chain Bridge and Horseshoe Falls

Outline Llangollen — Canal — Chain Bridge — Horseshoe Falls — Chain Bridge — Inman's Wood — Victoria Park — Llangollen.

Summary The first half of the walk is flat and easy along the canal towpath, yet it is full of interest. The canal passes through meadows, goes above the Eisteddfod field and above the railway. The Motor Museum, passed in a mile, displays mainly pre-war British cars and motorbikes. The clear water reveals perch and roach, especially under the shadow of the Chain Bridge Hotel. This hotel was named after the original bridge that led across the river to Berwyn Station; the present bouncy suspension bridge is the third bridge on the site.

After reaching the Horseshoe Falls, a slightly higher return route is taken to include spectacular views of the valley. An easy option for young children is to take the train to Berwyn and, after visiting the falls (sections 2 and 3), return along the towpath to Llangollen.

Attractions In Llangollen, ECTARC (the European Centre For Traditional And Regional Cultures) hold regular free exhibitions. It also has the world's largest Arthurian Library, containing hundreds of books based on the legends of King Arthur and his Knights of the Round Table. The nearby woollen mill is also open to visitors.

Llangollen Station with 'Thomas the Tank Engine' and a variety of special excursions fascinates both young and old. Nearby is the Bishop Trevor Bridge where you can look up- or down-stream to see the weirs that once raised the level of water to power the water-mills here.

Early summer brings musicians from all over the world to the International Eisteddfod held annually in July. Later on, daytrippers and holidaymakers arrive in profusion. The autumn torrents create an influx of canoeists risking their lives and limbs in the swirling white water of the River Dee/Afon Dyfrdwy. Flotillas of tame ducks can be seen all year round.

Refreshments Llangollen is full of cafés and restaurants of various types including Chinese, Indian, Pizza and Vegetarian. Halfway around the walk the Chain Bridge Hotel serves morning coffee, lunches and afternoon tea, but soft drinks are available only when the bar is open. Despite a sign near the hotel saying no picnicking, the towpath here which coincides with the driveway is a public footpath so you are legally allowed to sit at the water's edge and munch to your heart's content.

Route 1

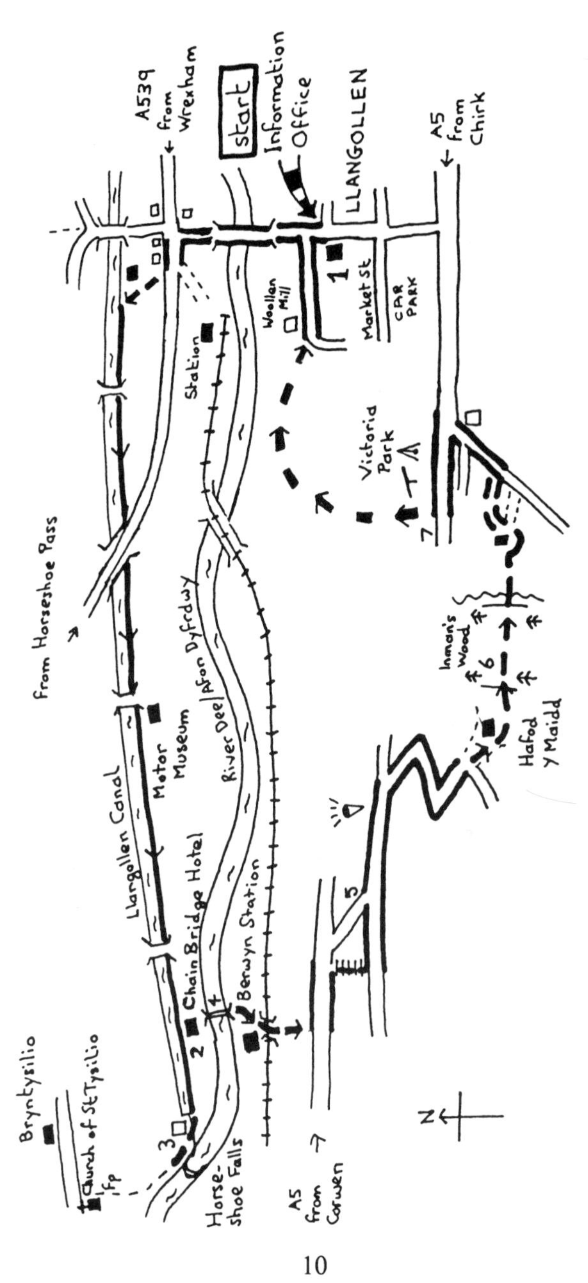

A539 from Wrexham
start
Information Office
LLANGOLLEN
A5 from Chirk
Market St
CAR PARK
Woollen Mill
Station
Victoria Park
Inman's Wood
Hafod Y Maidd
From Horseshoe Pass
Llangollen Canal
Motor Museum
River Dee
Afon Dyfrdwy
Chain Bridge Hotel
Berwyn Station
Horse-shoe Falls
A5 from Corwen
Brynytysilio
Church of St Tysilio
fp
N
1
2
3
4
5
6
7

Route 1

Chain Bridge and Horseshoe Falls 1¾ or 4 miles

START: *Llangollen Tourist Information Office G.R. SJ 214420. Buses go to Llangollen from Chester, Wrexham, Corwen, Bala and Barmouth, with occasional services from Chirk and Oswestry. A car park can be found in the town centre.*

Alternative *The short walk is made by catching the train from Llangollen to Berwyn, crossing the river (under the tunnel and across Chain Bridge) and then following sections 2 and 3. You then return from the Chain Bridge by canal towpath until you reach a point above Llangollen Station, where you descend to the town.*

ROUTE

1. *Cross the old bridge over the Dee in the town centre. Over the main road and slightly to your left, a sloped path takes you uphill on to the canal towpath. Turn left. Follow it for 1¾ miles, passing the Motor Museum, to reach the Chain Bridge Hotel.*
2. *Continue along the towpath past the hotel entrance. In a few hundred metres you reach the end of the canal. Just beyond is the weir, commonly known as Horseshoe Falls. (The pleasant path goes only a little farther until it heads away from the river to Llantysilio Church and the road.) Above the meadow is Bryntisilio, a Georgian house with Italianate styling.*
3. *Return along the canal towpath to Chain Bridge.*
4. *Unless you wish to return to Llangollen along the towpath or by train, you should now cross Chain Bridge and ascend to the busy road. Turn left and, just before a lane, cross over and climb the steps on your right. Turn left at the top.*
5. *Ignore the turning back to the main road but fork right at the next junction and, at the third bend, continue straight on through a farm, Hafod y Maidd. Fork right in the farmyard and go over the stile. Continue straight ahead through Inman's Wood (replanted in 1991).*
6. *The path leads next to a cottage. Continue along the drive for a few metres then fork right on to a track. At the tarmac lane, turn left and descend to the main road.*
7. *Turn left and immediately right through the iron kissing-gate. Go through the children's playground to follow the riverside terrace back to the town centre.*

WHITE WATER AT LLANGOLLEN

Route 2 **3 miles**

Castell Dinas Brân

Outline Llangollen — Canal — Fourways — Dinas Brân — Llangollen.

Summary Almost every guide book in North Wales seems to include a route up Dinas Brân even though the castle is obvious from the town. Yet I still meet a large number of people who have not climbed this romantic peak. The usual route is up the face of the hill but I have chosen a slightly easier way around the valley at its foot, and then up the waymarked path between the Trevor Rocks of Eglwyseg Escarpment (those snowy limestone crags overlooking the town) and the castle. The route is still steep, and you are warned that the grassy sheep-cropped path can be extremely slippery after wet weather or heavy dew. If in doubt, the safest way up and down is on all fours. You are also warned to keep children away from the edges of the castle, especially in windy weather.

Attractions From the castle on Dinas Brân, Llangollen is laid out in front of you like a map. Look for the church dedicated to St Collen (Llan = church, gollen = Collen); and the River Dee/Afon Dyfrdwy as landmarks and see what else you can spot as the noisy traffic becomes just a layout of matchbox cars and the steam train a whistle echoing in the hills.

The stone castle was inhabited by Welsh princes in Norman times and later destroyed by the Welsh as they retreated from Edward I's army. Although garrisoned by the English, the new lord decided to live closer to the English border at Holt Castle and left this one to decay.

See if you can find the main gate with its two guard houses; the keep, a former two-storey building still showing the slots where a staircase was situated; and the apsidal (D-shaped) tower. The rest must be left to your imagination as the only detailed archaeological study discovered little. What can be seen are the remaining ramparts of an Iron Age hillfort around the eastern slopes of the castle.

An English name for Castell Dinas Brân is Crow Castle (although an early 19th century visitor recorded it as Croak Castle). This is a literal translation of bran, which means crow or raven, and these birds were used in at least one poem about the ruin:

> Now no-one will wend from the fields of the fight
> To the fortress on high, save the raven and the crow.

Castell and dinas are both Welsh words for fortress.

Refreshments Take your own sandwiches or refresh yourself in one of the town's many cafés.

Route 2

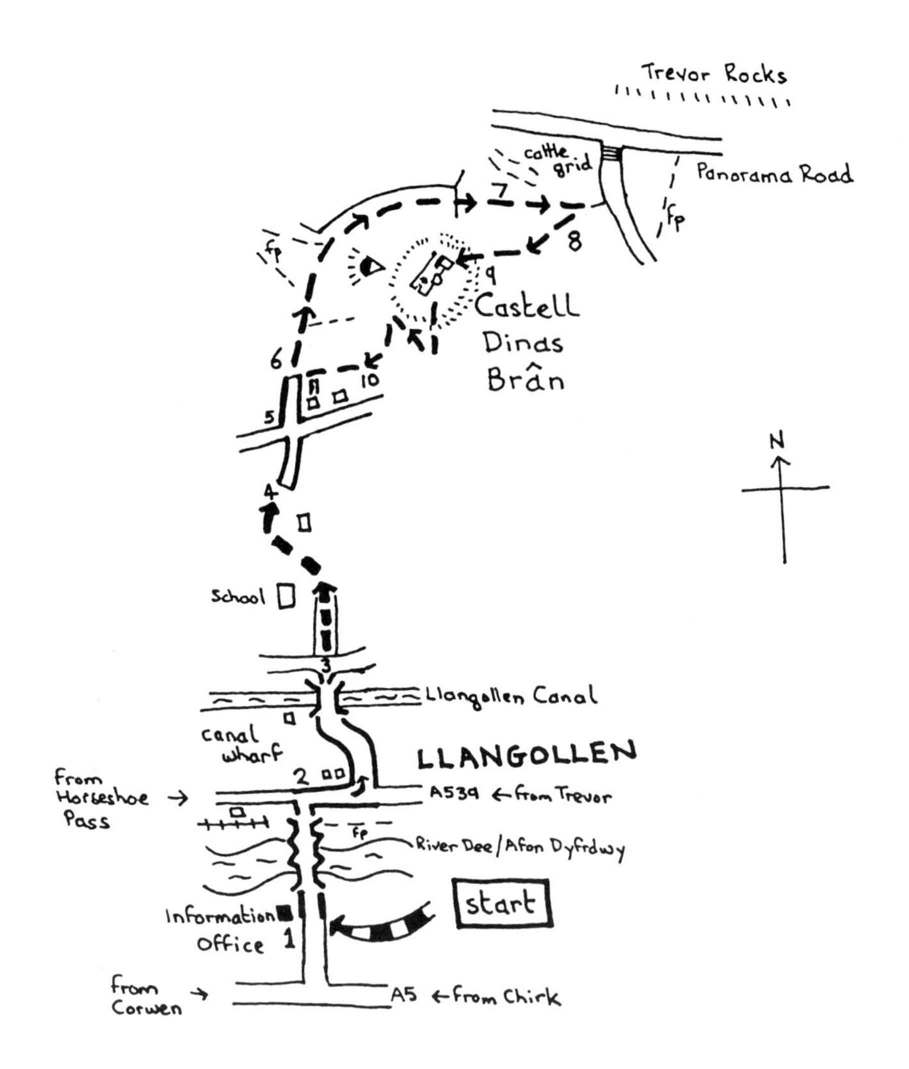

Trevor Rocks
cattle grid
Panorama Road
fp
fp
7
8
9
Castell Dinas Brân
6
10
5
4
N
School
3
Llangollen Canal
canal wharf
LLANGOLLEN
From Horseshoe Pass
2
A539 ← from Trevor
fp
River Dee/Afon Dyfrdwy
start
Information Office
1
from Corwen
A5 ← from Chirk

Route 2

Castell Dinas Brân — 3 miles

START: *Llangollen Tourist Information Office G.R.SJ 214420. Buses go to Llangollen from Chester, Wrexham, Corwen, Bala and Barmouth with occasional services from Chirk and Oswestry. A car park can be found in the town centre.*

ROUTE

1. *From the Tourist Information Office cross the old stone bridge over the River Dee/Afon Dyfrdwy.*
2. *Turn right at the T-junction then first left.*
3. *Cross the canal bridge and take the path ahead.*
4. *Above the enclosed path and the winding meadow path, join a track.*
5. *When you reach the four-way junction continue ahead.*
6. *Go through the kissing-gate and take the lower (left-hand) path around the hill but ignore paths down to the left and one up to the castle.*
7. *Continue over a stile. When you reach the road, you can cross the stile and turn left to extend your walk along the Panorama Road as far as you wish, returning across the roadside stile to continue the main route.*
8. *Turn right (left if you are coming back from the extension) and climb the waymarked path to the summit of Dinas Brân.*
9. *After looking around the castle descend the zig-zag path towards Llangollen.*
10. *Do not take a stile on your left but continue over the small hump to find the kissing-gate.*
11. *Retrace your steps (ahead at the junctions) to Llangollen.*

LLANGOLLEN STATION

Route 3 **2 or 3 miles**

Above Llangollen

Outline Llangollen — River Dee — Victoria Park — fields and lanes — Plas Newydd — Llangollen.

Summary This route takes you along the river bank and through the park. If your children will let you go any farther the main walk then skirts the top of the town with a steep climb on an old bridleway, or an easy alternative along a lane. Both routes then follow a short woodland path which leads between lanes on the way to Plas Newydd.

Attractions Only a short climb through two fields is needed for a panorama of the town and mountains. This is an ideal stop for a picnic, but please stay on the path and leave no litter. A shallow stream passed on the downward journey is a good place to stop for smaller children. Once again, you may not be able to get away as they amuse themselves with a variety of rocks and stones in crystal clear water at the start of an old mill-leat.

The gardens of Plas Newydd are open to the public all year; the house in summer only. Children will love the inside of this building which was lovingly arranged by the two 'Ladies of Llangollen' who lived here in the early 19th century.

Lady Eleanor Butler and Sarah Ponsonby eloped here in 1778 and the house gained a wealth of internal and external embellishments until Sarah Ponsonby died in 1831. The history of these two eccentrics, who were visited by Wedgwood, Wordsworth and the Duke of Wellington among other notables, and became a legend in their own lifetime, has been well documented in two Penguin books by Elizabeth Mavor (for sale in the Information Centre). A summary of their lives can also be found inside the house, now a museum and, in my guide to Pengwern Vale (also at the Information Centre).

General Yorke, related to the Yorkes of Erddig (see later walks in this book), eventually bought the house and added on two wings which have since, unfortunately, been demolished.

Refreshments There are several places where a picnic could be eaten on the route: one is mentioned in the directions, another is Plas Newydd. At the foot of the hill, on the way back from Plas Newydd, the Simla Indian Restaurant usually opens about 7pm but it is wise to book a table first (0978 860610).

Route 3

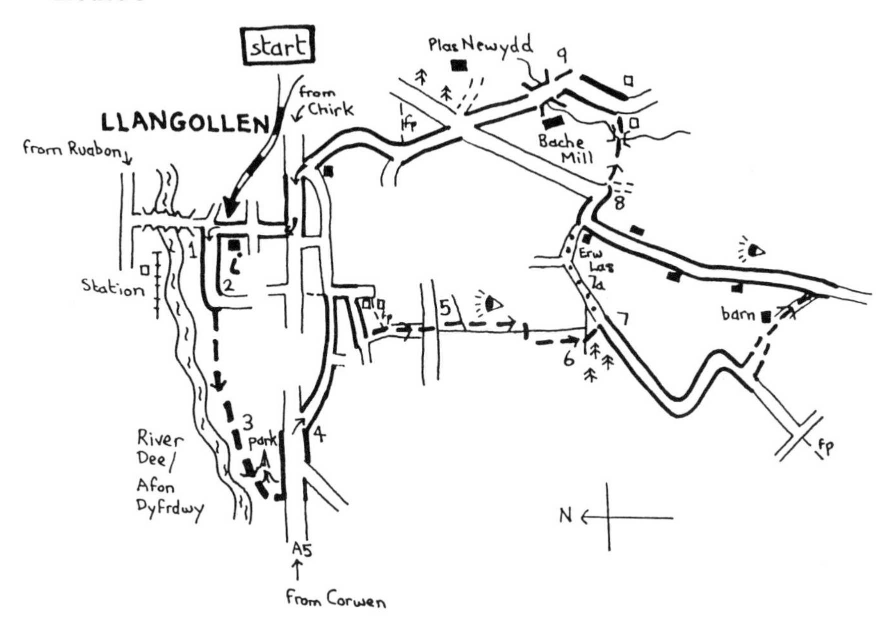

THOMAS THE TANK ENGINE

Route 3

Above Llangollen — 2 or 3 miles

START: *Llangollen Tourist Information Office G.R. SJ 214420. Buses go to Llangollen from Chester, Wrexham, Corwen, Bala and Barmouth with occasional services from Chirk and Oswestry. A car park can be found in the town centre.*

Alternative *For the longer and steeper route follow 7. For the easy route follow 7a.*

ROUTE

1. *From the Tourist Information Office in the centre of Llangollen turn towards the river and immediately turn left into the next street.*
2. *Follow this street to the corner then take the riverside terrace ahead.*
3. *When you reach the park turn left to the main road. Turn left again (to face the town) and fork up the second right turn.*
4. *Take the second right turn (Pen-y-bryn) and immediately fork right up the drive. Take the first path on the left and then ignore the left fork.*
5. *Cross the lane and two stiles. Take another stile to cross into the field on your right but continue uphill, now with the hedge on your left.*
6. *Beyond the next stile, climb to the track.*
7. *For the longer, steeper route, turn right and climb half a mile to the track junction. Turn left and follow this track towards a corrugated-iron barn. Take the gate on your right to keep this barn on your left. Continue to the lane and turn downhill. Ignoring a left turn after three farms, continue to a sharp left bend.*

7a. *For the shorter route, turn left. At the lane fork right to the T-junction below a house 'Erw Las' where you turn left and continue to a sharp left bend.*

8. *From this sharp bend, go ahead down the footpath, crossing a stream and the start of an old mill-leat. Turn left at the lane.*
9. *Another left turn puts you on the lane leading back to the town. On your way you pass the old mill on your left (private property) and Plas Newydd on your right (open to the public).*

WOODLAND PATH

Route 4 **4 miles**

Pen-llan-y-gŵr

Outline Bwlchgwyn — Coed Mawr — Avenue Wood — Nant Wood — Black Wood — Coed Mawr — Bwlchgwyn.

Summary The four woods that this route passes through are virtually indistinguishable as separate entities nowadays. A steady ascent is made along forest tracks up the side of Pen-llan-y-gŵr where the climb is rewarded by views of the nearby Welsh valleys and the Cheshire plain. You then descend into Nant Wood before gradually climbing up the valley, Nant-y-Ffrith, to Bwlchgwyn.

Attractions From time immemorial walkers have enjoyed views of the valley and have descended a steep path to the interesting 'Wedding Cave' and waterfall here. Earlier this century a wedding reception is said to have been held within and until recently a set of concrete steps was in evidence. A postcard showing the view from the foot of the path was sold locally.

However, in their wisdom, the Forestry Commission have now decided that the path is too steep and have erected a sign and fence to make the point clear. Local people have stood up for their rights and ignore the sign and regularly remove the fence. Unfortunately the path is not a definitive right of way and although reliable evidence has been collected as to the past use of the path over the necessary 20 years to make it legally public, this evidence cannot be taken into consideration as the land is owned by the Commission as Crown Property. Whilst I cannot recommend that you take the path to the cave and have left it off the main route, I am equally loath not to put the facts before you and therefore show its position on the map. The path is certainly steep but my four year old managed it with relative ease. It can be difficult in wet weather.

As you proceed on the main route you pass the former coach house (now a private residence) of the Nant y Frith Estate.

In 1850 a Liverpool tea merchant built a hunting lodge on the estate and, after being bought by another merchant, it was sold, in 1865, to a Mr Kyrke, an entrepreneur who built the imposing Nant y Frith Hall about halfway up the hillside. His son inherited the estate in 1883 but by 1950 the Bwlchgwyn Roadstone Company owned the estate, and the Hall had been demolished. All that remains is this coach house, the stone bridge, and some of the ornamental trees that were planted last century. The hall site, shown on the map, is popular for picnics.

At the highest point on the route is a set of rocks ideal for children to scramble on. As you leave the wood and enter the fields look for the remains

continued on page 23

Route 4

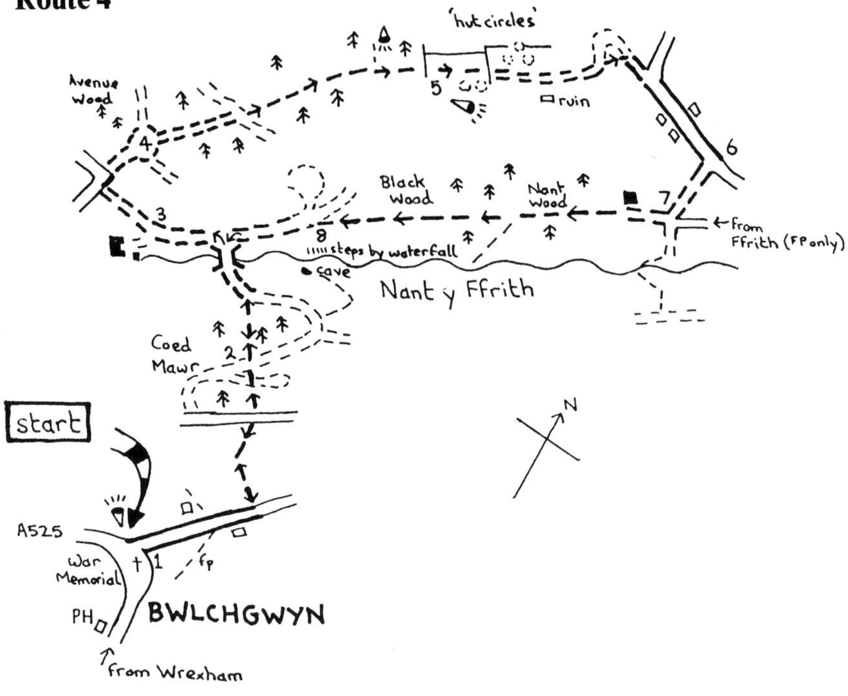

ELEVATION

Route 4

Pen-llan-y-gŵr **4 miles**

START: *Bwlchgwyn War Memorial, A525 G.R. SJ 263536. Buses go to Bwlchgwyn from Wrexham. Cars may be parked by the War Memorial.*

ROUTE

1. *From the War Memorial turn down the lane. After 200 yards take the path down to the left. Cross the lane and continue to the second forest track. (Down to your right, from the corner of the track is the old path to the cave and waterfalls.)*
2. *Your route continues across the forest track and down the path. Cross the bridge and turn left.*
3. *Fork right before the house. At the lane turn right then, where the lane bends sharp left, follow the track ahead.*
4. *At the large clearing take the central green path and, in less than half a mile, cross the forest track. (On leaving the firs there is a rocky viewpoint to your right.)*
5. *When you emerge from the forest continue ahead over 2 stiles, passing the hut circles on both sides. Follow the track to the lane.*
6. *Six hundred metres downhill turn right along the open green bridleway.*
7. *At the crossing path turn right and, beyond the house, follow the clear path for a mile ignoring the left fork unless you want to go down to the stream.*
8. *When you meet the wide forest track, fork left downhill. Cross the stone bridge and retrace your steps to the War Memorial.*

---

of prehistoric 'hut circles' on both sides of the path. Might these have been some of the first man-made thatched houses in this country? Living in these pits within the womb of mother earth, the people here probably took sustenance from father sun by having the hut entrances opening to the southeast: the direction of the sun during the colder months of the year.

Refreshments The rocks or the Hall site are both ideal spots for a picnic. Please leave no litter in these pleasant woodlands. There is a shop in Bwlchgwyn.

PONTCYSYLLTE AQUEDUCT

Route 5 **¾, 2 or 4 miles**

Ty Mawr and Pontcysyllte Aqueduct

Outline Ty Mawr Country Park — Pontcysyllte Aqueduct — Froncysyllte — Tan-y-cut — Irish Bridge — Newbridge — Ty Mawr.

Summary After looking around Ty Mawr you follow the bank of the River Dee/Afon Dyfrdwy to the canal basin before crossing Telford's 'Stream in the Sky'—an aqueduct carrying the Llangollen Canal. (An alternative is given for those who would prefer to look up at the high bridge from ground level.) The route then goes along the towpath past a small nature reserve and follows the former main road back to the park.

Attractions Tame sheep, horses, donkeys, goats and hens can be found in the country park, as well as an information centre focused towards children. The variety of events throughout the year are also organised with children in mind. (Phone the Park Rangers on 0978 822780 for up-to-date information.) The river and canalside walk appeals to most people and none can fail to be exhilarated by the aqueduct crossing. Remember there is a lower alternative.

Tan-y-cut Wood, associated with the country park, has a nature walk for the would-be botanist, but look out for unusual wild flowers all around the route. If children are interested, remember to take a field guide on the walk and not to take plants home for identification: many plants live in a fragile environment and their removal spoils the enjoyment of others and is, in any case, illegal.

Irish Bridge was named after the Irish 'navvies' (navigation workers) who cut this canal in the early 19th century using only hand-tools and horse-power, before lining it with clay 'puddle' to keep in the water.

Views encompass five bridges in the valley which carry water, rail and road from four centuries of changing transportation methods. Below the aqueduct is the stone bridge dating from the 17th century. The new bridge which carries the bypass (A483) can be seen on the return journey while you cross the older 'Newbridge' and can look down from this on the piers of the even older bridge that carried the toll road across the Dee. The railway viaduct, built by Henry Robertson for the Great Western Railway in 1848, features on the country park logo. Unfortunately, steam trains are rarely seen on it now, the regular route being covered by a small diesel paytrain.

Refreshments Except on event days there are no refreshments available at the Country Park. However, 'The Telford Inn' near the aqueduct has seats outside overlooking the canal basin; the inn welcomes families and has a

continued on page 27

Route 5

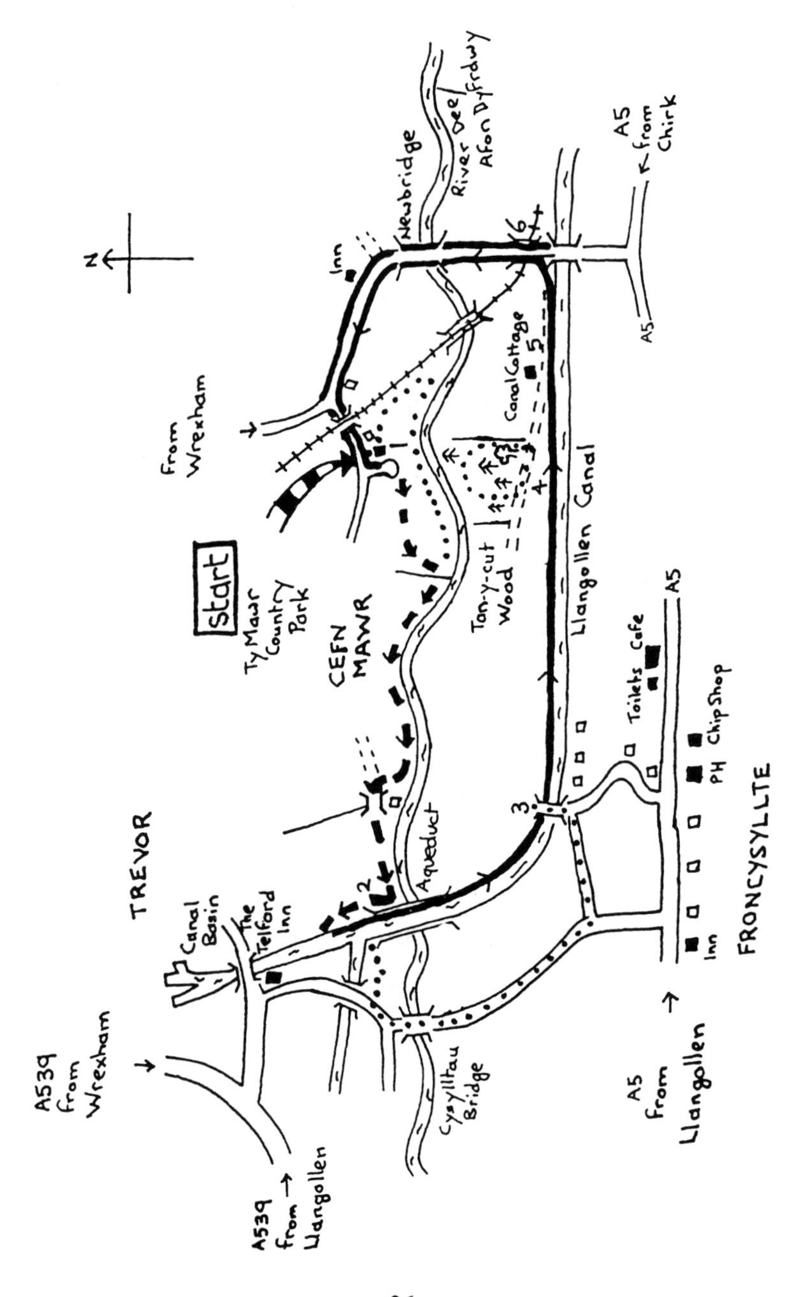

N
Start
Ty Mawr Country Park
CEFN MAWR
TREVOR
Canal Basin
The Telford Inn
Aqueduct
Cysylltau Bridge
A539 from Wrexham
A539 from → Llangollen
From Wrexham
Inn
Newbridge
River Dee
Afon Dyfrdwy
A5 from Chirk
A5
Canal Cottage
Tan-y-cut Wood
Llangollen Canal
Toilets
Cafe
Chip Shop
PH
Inn
FRONCYSYLLTE
A5 from Llangollen
1
2
3
4
5
6

Route 5

Ty Mawr and Pontcysyllte Aqueduct ¾, 2 or 4 miles

START: *Ty Mawr Country Park near Newbridge G.R.SJ 284414. Regular buses on the Wrexham–Oswestry, Wrexham–Cefn, and Wrexham–Llangollen services. Car parking available.*

Alternatives *A short walk of less than a mile can be made by following the circular path within the country park. Returning from the aqueduct by the same riverside path shortens the walk to 2 miles. The high aqueduct crossing may be avoided by following the path under the aqueduct, turning left, crossing the stone bridge and going up the lane, then rejoining the canal and crossing the lift bridge.*

ROUTE

1. *From the foot of the car park in the country park turn right following the signs 'Country Park Walk and Aqueduct'. Near the river bank take the stepped footpath to your right. This clear path eventually turns left along a track behind a red brick pumphouse. Continue along the river bank to the aqueduct piers.*
2. *Climb the steps and turn right. After looking at the canal basin, swing bridge and dock on your right, cross the aqueduct.*
3. *Follow the towpath to a lift bridge (one of many on this canal designed to resemble the original wooden lift bridges of the early 19th century). Visitors to the village should cross the bridge and fork left up the lane; a café and public conveniences are 200 metres to your left along the main road.*
4. *The main route continues along the towpath. In half a mile, where the concrete canal bank narrows, look out for a stile on the track below the canal. This is the entrance to the circular nature trail around Tan-y-cut Wood.*
5. *Continue along the towpath to the overhead road bridge: Irish Bridge.*
6. *Turn left along the road and follow it for half a mile, crossing the river and turning under the first railway bridge on your left, back to the country park.*

---

children's menu, as well as catering for vegetarians. Halfway around the walk, the village of Froncysyllte boasts a café, a chip shop, two inns and public conveniences.

NAVIGATION

Route 6 **3½ or 4 miles**

Nant Mill and Bersham Iron Works

Outline Nant Mill — Plas Power Woods — Bersham Ironworks — Bersham Heritage Centre — Old Railway Line — Cadwgan — Nant Mill.

Summary An easy walk gently downhill through the fascinating Plas Power woodland is followed by a short road walk to Bersham Ironworks and the Bersham Heritage Centre. The return journey takes you along a dismantled railway line, now a wildlife habitat, and across fields beside the 8th century earthwork, Offa's Dyke.

Attractions Nant Mill was a corn mill built in 1832 for the local estate. It was one of two or three mills that worked here in different ages. The mill is now a Visitor Centre and short guides to the plants and ruins in the area are available inside.

There is a small admission charge, but for this you and your children can explore the underground life of a mole, take bark rubbings or just find out about the local wildlife.

The walk through Plas Power Wood, now owned by the Woodland Trust, is on a flat track which I rediscovered after it had been completely overgrown for some years. Luckily, one of the first people to walk the track before it had been cleared, was an archaeologist who recognised it as a possible tramway.

My further research revealed sections of the trackbed for much of the length of the valley: from Minera mines to the former turnpike road at Felin Puleston. Meanwhile at Bersham Ironworks the archaeologists dug up wooden tramway rails and at Bersham Industrial Heritage Centre an old plan of the ironworks revealed the entrance of the 'Waggonway or Railroad'.

The tramway path cuts through a section of Offa's Dyke and now that the trees have been cleared from its banks one can appreciate the enormity of this defensive ditch and embankment which, for a short time during the 8th century, was the border of England and Wales. Once again more information is available at the Nant Mill Visitor Centre.

Archaeologists are still stripping back the layers of history from the Bersham Ironworks where 'Iron Mad' John Wilkinson first used coke to smelt iron. Continue to the Bersham Industrial Heritage Centre to find out more about this amazing man and some of the products which he made. Wilkinson even produced his own coinage which his workers could only spend at his shops, as well as his own cast-iron coffin!

The return journey follows another industrial relic: a dismantled

continued on page 32

Route 6

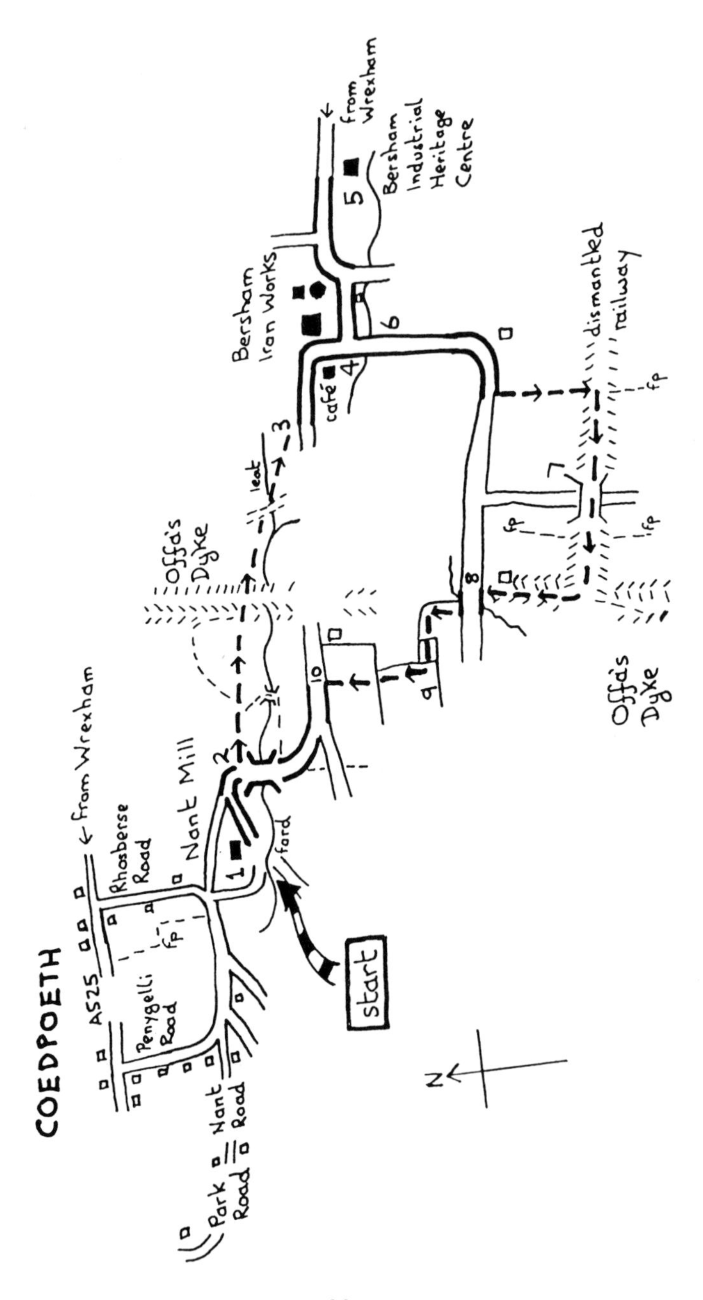

COEDPOETH
A525
Penygelli Road
Rhosberse Road
← from Wrexham
Nant Mill
Park Road
Nant Road
fp
ford
start
1
2
Offa's Dyke
leat
3
café
4
Bersham Iron Works
5
Bersham Industrial Heritage Centre
from Wrexham
6
dismantled railway
fp
7
fp
8
Offa's Dyke
9
10
N

Route 6

Nant Mill and Bersham Iron Works — 3½ or 4 miles

START: *Nant Mill Visitor Centre G.R.SJ 289501. Car parking on site. Follow the A525 from Wrexham Bypass to the first houses in the village of Coedpoeth. Turn left along Rhosberse Road to the mill. Buses from Wrexham and Minera go through Coedpoeth, from where you should follow Park Road and its continuation, Nant Road, to Nant Mill.*

Alternative *The slightly shorter walk is made by missing out sections 4 and 5, thus not visiting the Bersham Industrial Heritage Centre.*

ROUTE

1. *From the mill door go up the lane to the junction. Turn right downhill.*
2. *Go through the kissing-gate before the bridge and follow the woodland 'tramway' path for a mile, passing Offa's Dyke and Plas Power Chapel.*
3. *When you join the lane, continue in the same direction to Bersham Ironworks and Mill Farm House.*
4. *Turn left at the road junction beside the Ironworks and left again at the main road to find the Bersham Industrial Heritage Centre in 100 metres or so.*
5. *Return to the Ironworks entrance and turn left by the houses.*
6. *Follow the lane ahead and continue onto the signed footpath. Follow this well-worn path to climb the disused railway embankment. Turn right.*
7. *Cross a bridge and pass a set of steps but when the path ends at a dismantled bridge take the slope down to the field. Turn right and follow the field boundary, part of Offa's Dyke, to the lane.*
8. *Turn left, then beyond the stream take the stile beside a gate on your right. Now follow the field boundary halfway around the field to take the bridge and stile into woodland. Continue ahead.*
9. *In the next field turn right and, at the corner, go ahead across the hump of another field, by the telegraph pole, to a stone stile.*
10. *Turn left along the lane then fork right at the junction. Nant Mill is half a mile ahead.*

mineral railway that served the mines and quarries this side of Ruabon mountain.

Refreshments Take your own picnic to Nant Mill where tables are provided beside the River Clywedog, or visit Mill Farm House, now a restaurant and tea room, opposite the Ironworks halfway around your route. See the appendices for phone and opening details.

KING'S MILL AND BRICK KILN

Route 7 **1 or 3 miles**

King's Mill and Afon Clywedog

Outline King's Mill — Erddig — Bryn-y-cabanau — King's Mill.

Summary An easy walk starting at the converted mill and meandering through the riverside meadows of Erddig Park. In winter the tunnel path leading from the mill under the A525 to Erddig occasionally floods and you may have to cross the road instead. The first part of the walk is suitable for pushchairs and has been the course of a popular Rambler's Association Family Ramble. The return is on slightly higher ground through field and woodland.

There is an option to extend the walk by two miles before you cross the river.

Attractions King's Mill is now a Visitor Centre, open most of the year and run by Wrexham Maelor Borough Council. (See the appendices for details and telephone number.) Inside can be found a turning water-wheel. The mill had two when it was working and the remaining centre of the other is visible.

While you listen to the miller tell his story, you can see his implements around him. Then go upstairs to see an exhibition about the mill, and a video showing the story of the Clywedog Valley, its former mills and industries. Behind the mill is an old brick kiln.

Erddig Park has been open to the public for over two centuries thanks to the generosity of its former owners, the Yorke family. It was finally given to the National Trust by the last Squire Yorke within his lifetime. Look for the 1779 proclamation on the Country Park display board.

The Afon (river) Clywedog is shallow in summer and, as it now has no industries upstream, is as safe as any for children to play in.

The Clywedog Valley was once the industrial heart of the area with over 19 mills using water power to run a variety of industrial activities. This guide includes four walks in the valley, each with a view of former industry. Once you have the feel of the valley try following the Ordnance Survey Pathfinder Maps for the area, available from bookshops, or the 'Walks Around Wrexham Maelor' series on sale at the local information office or the town reference library.

Refreshments The riverside is an ideal area for picnics but please take all your litter home with you.

Route 7

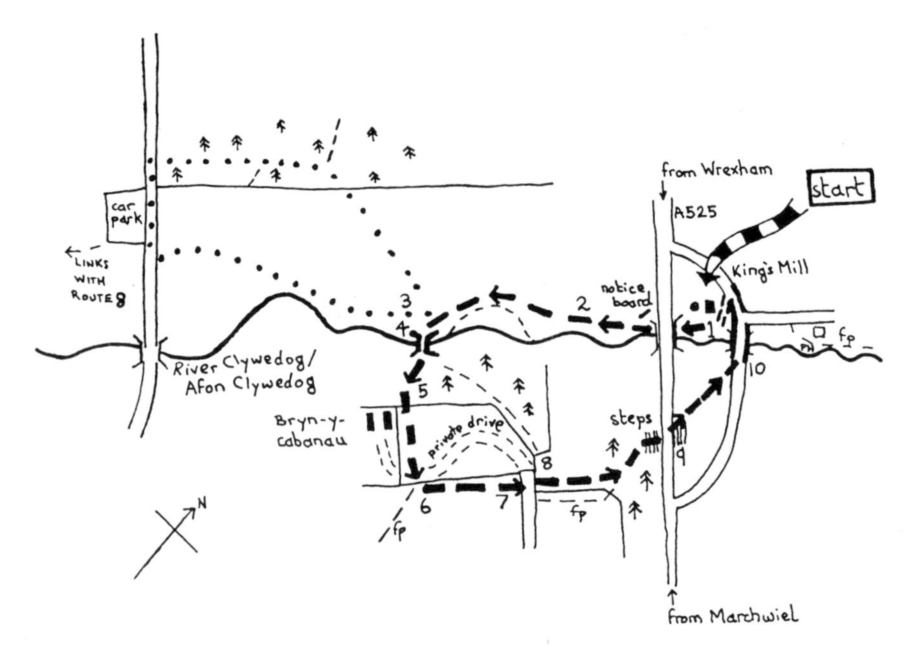

EXPLORATION

Route 7

King's Mill and Afon Clywedog 1 or 3 miles

START: *King's Mill, Wrexham G.R. SJ 347492. Buses from Wrexham to Marchwiel pass King's Mill. By car follow the A525 Whitchurch road for less than a mile from Wrexham town centre.*

Alternative *Extend the walk using section 3. For the short walk miss out this section.*

ROUTE

1. *Head upstream, alongside the Afon (river) Clywedog, going under the road bridge.*
2. *Continue along the riverside to the footbridge.*
3. *An extension to the route can be made here by continuing alongside the river to the next road and returning to this bridge by turning right and right again onto the woodland path on the far side of this meadow.*
4. *Cross the footbridge and follow the clear path to the right.*
5. *Just past a beech tree with three trunks take the upper left fork to a stile behind buildings, then continue in the same direction to another stile.*
6. *Turn left and follow the field boundary to the field corner.*
7. *Cross the track and take the stile on your left.*
8. *Ignore a stile on your left (this path leads back to the footbridge). In 250 metres climb steps to the road.*
9. *On the other side descend similar steps and bear half-left across the field, to the gateway.*
10. *Turn left to King's Mill.*

LLANTYSILIO CHURCH (Route 1)

Route 8 **2 or 3 miles**

Erdigg: Cup and Saucer

Outline Felin Puleston — River Clywedog — Erddig — Cup and Saucer — Felin Puleston.

Summary A flat and pleasant walk through meadows followed by a short climb to the house at Erddig. The return is along the river bank.

Attractions The Visitor Centre or Agricultural Museum at Felin Puleston is temporarily closed at the time of writing but some early combine harvesters can be seen outside. Nearby, the wide kissing-gates give pushchair and wheelchair access to the wildflower meadow. Sturdy pushchairs can be used on this walk if you proceed on the other bank of the river.

There is an abundance of plant life through Erddig. Take a field guide in spring or summer to identify the plants and trees. Among the plants, look for ox-eye daisy, field speedwell, crosswort, Japanese knotweed, comfrey, burdock, raspberry, two types of buttercup, and many different grasses. Trees include hazel, alder, beech, oak, wellingtonia, cedar of Lebanon and monkey puzzle. There are also a variety of birds and animals: rabbit, grey squirrel, kingfisher and jay were some of the ones I saw last time I visited.

Big Wood, above the river, was the site of a Norman castle: a wooden motte and bailey similar to those depicted on the famous Bayeux Tapestry. The castle of 'Wristlesham' (Wrexham) was listed in the pipe rolls of 1161.

Look inside the dovecote door to see the stone roosts where, amongst the white doves, the occasional crow and pigeon have taken up residence.

When you reach the herb garden rub your hands lightly over the plants; smell and try to recognise the many scents: marjoram, thyme, lovage, sage, alexanders, fennel, borage and sweet cicely are amongst those present.

The times of entry to the grounds and house are given in the appendices. Leave plenty of time if you wish to visit both.

The original house dates from the late 17th century and was remodelled in the 18th by John Mellor. In 1733 Simon Yorke inherited the estate, and it was finally given to the National Trust in 1973. The damage caused by years of neglect and mining subsidence was partly repaired before the house was opened by the Prince of Wales in 1977. Volunteer work in the house and grounds still continues.

The 'cup and saucer' is an ornamental weir that was built in 1774. Nearby is the domed brick roof of an hydraulic-pump house.

continued on page 39

Route 8

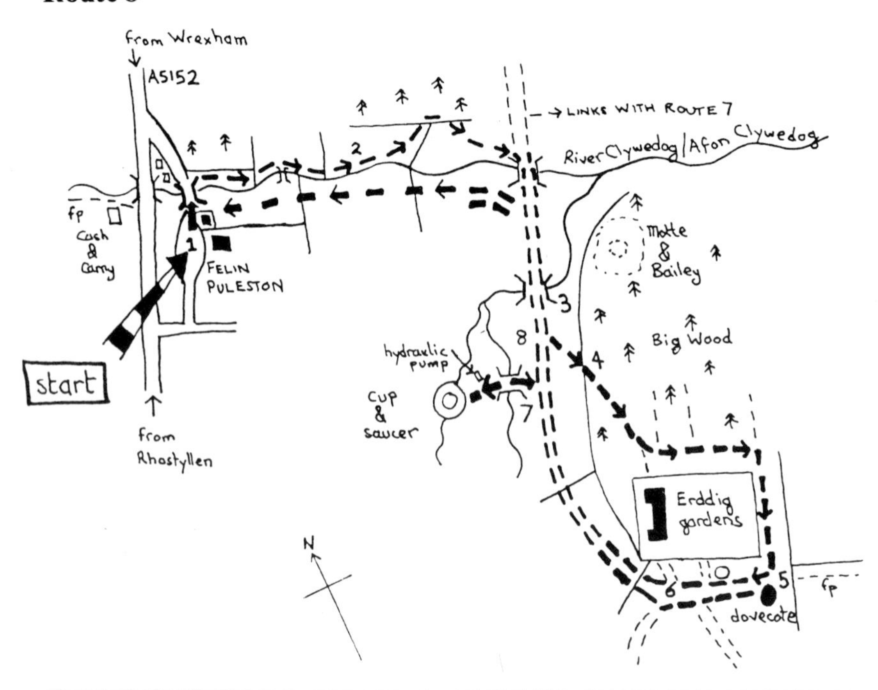

CONSIDERATION

Route 8

Erddig: Cup and Saucer — 2 or 3 miles

START: *Felin Puleston, 'Erddig Country Park car park'. G.R. SJ 376493. Buses from Wrexham to Rhos, Penycae, Cefn, Llangollen and Oswestry all pass Felin Puleston. By car Erddig is well-signposted with an acorn symbol. From the main road (and the bus stop) take the lane to Erddig and turn first left.*

Alternative *Return from the 'Cup and Saucer' by missing out sections 4, 5 and 6, thus not visiting the house at Erddig.*

ROUTE

1. *From the red-brick cottage, cross the bridge and turn right alongside the plantation and through the wildflower meadows. Keep to the riverside path.*
2. *Continue along the riverside, eventually entering woodland but soon leaving it again to cross the stone bridge on your right.*
3. *After crossing another stone bridge, but before the wooden bridge on your right, find an iron kissing-gate on your left.*
4. *Ascend the main woodland path (unless you want to explore Big Wood to your left) and keep right at all possible junctions to skirt the walled garden of Erddig.*
5. *Beyond the dovecote is the entrance and, even if you do not wish to visit the house, gardens, or café, you may look at the pond and herb garden outside the wall, then return to the driveway.*
6. *Follow the drive and turn second right, signposted 'Cup and Saucer'.*
7. *At the foot of the hill cross the wooden bridge on your left.*
8. *Retrace your steps to the track. Turn left. Cross the stone bridge, but before the next stone bridge over the Clywedog turn left and follow the riverside path to Felin Puleston.*

Refreshments The banks of the Clywedog are ideal for picnics, but please take your litter home. The café in Erddig is only available to NT members or by paying to visit the grounds. Before or after the walk there are a variety of cafés in nearby Wrexham. I particularly recommend the mushroom biryani at Amantola Tandoori, meals at Pizza Chef (still open after other pizza parlours have come and gone) and the beanburger at Burger King.

CITY ENGINE HOUSE

Route 9 **2 miles**

Esclusham Mountain and the City Arms

Outline Minera —The City Arms — New Brighton — Esclusham Mountain — New Brighton — Minera.

Summary Parts of this walk can be difficult and tiring in summer when the bracken almost completely covers the path. However my 4 year old did it without too much of a problem and still had energy to play on the variety of equipment at the City Arms. The beginning and the end of the walk are easy on a surfaced path.

If you take a dog on this walk remember that the mountain slopes are used for sheep grazing. Farmers here have regular problems with uncontrolled dogs and are quite legally entitled to shoot your dog if it appears to be threatening stock.

Attractions Millions of pounds have been spent on land reclamation at the Minera lead mines site. The poisonous lead wastes have been covered with plastic and topsoil while the old mine buildings are being preserved as a part of the Clywedog Valley 'Country Park'.

The 'City' or Meadow Shaft pithead buildings are prominent on the reclaimed site. The building once housed a large Cornish Engine which pumped water from the low-level mine. The shaft was the deepest in the area.

Lead mining in the area dates back probably to Roman times and there are records of mining just north of here in the 13th and 14th centuries. However, after a Chester butcher left his land here to 'the poor of every Company of Merchants and Craftsmen of Chester' the lease was taken up by a Mayor of Chester who was also a silversmith. Over 10,000 tons of lead ore (which also contains silver) were extracted in 20 years.

In the early 19th century nearly five times as much ore was mined from the pits in Minera, while John Wilkinson quarried limestone from the head of the valley for his Iron Works at Bersham and probably transported it down a 'Waggonway' or tramway lying to the rear of the City Arms.

At the end of the 19th century the Minera Lead Mining Company built their own lead smelting works. The foot of its once tall chimney can be seen below the track leading to the mountain. The upper part was demolished in World War II to stop enemy planes using it as a sighting point.

The City Arms is named after the Chester Charities; several boundary stones in the area bear the name of Owen Jones, the butcher who originally bequeathed the land.

On the way down the lane from the mountain look for a small ruin on

continued on page 42

Route 9

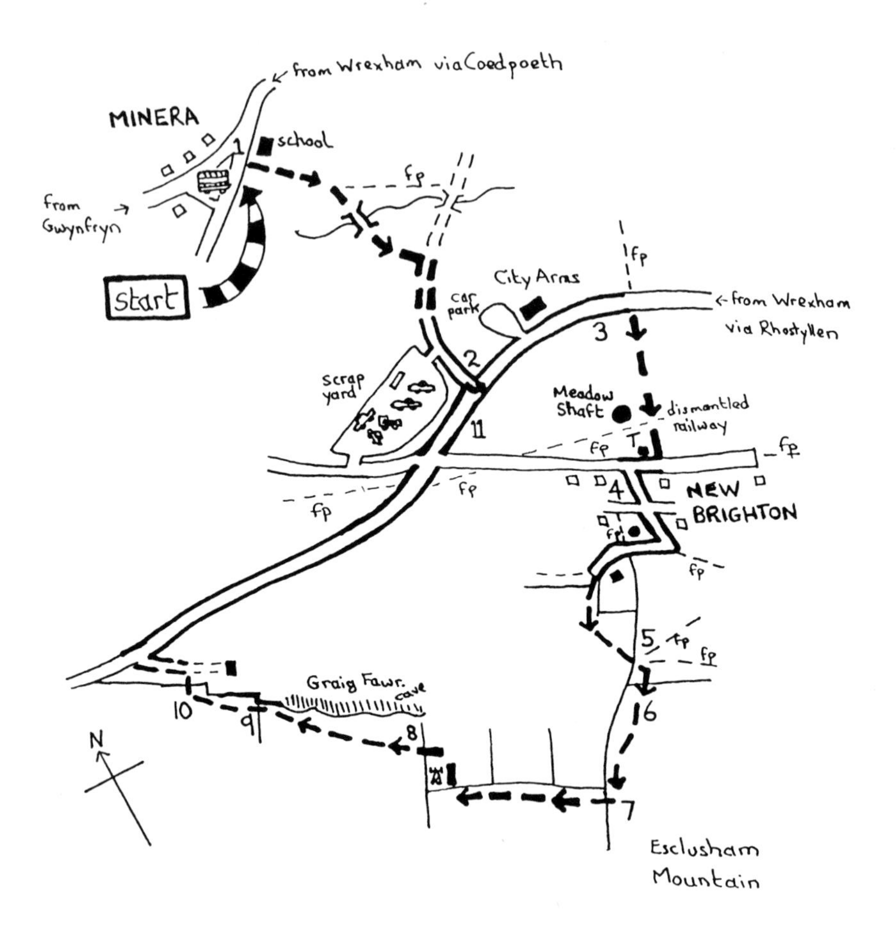

your left—this was a smithy which also served as a mortuary for miners who received fatal injuries in the area.

Refreshments The City Arms has a family room inside and also tables outside in or near the play area. A wide choice of meals, including vegetarian dishes, are served lunchtimes and evenings.

Route 9

Esclusham Mountain and the City Arms — 2 miles

START: *Minera bus terminus G.R. SJ 272518. Buses from Wrexham.*

Alternative *There are no car parks near the bus stop but permission has been given for you to park at the City Arms G.R. SJ 274511 for a shorter walk. Just miss out directions 1, 2 & 11.*

ROUTE

1. *From the bus stop cross the road and follow the path down beside the school. Do not fork left but continue over the bridge, turning right when you meet the track.*
2. *At the main road turn left to the City Arms.*
3. *Continue to the path on your right and head up past the pithead buildings to the lane. You should emerge by a telephone box.*
4. *Take the uphill lane almost opposite. Continue to the top. Beyond the house, go over the stile and follow the boundary on your left. Beyond the rear of the garden turn half-left to cross a wooden stile in the drystone wall.*
5. *Turn almost immediately right to cross another stile.*
6. *Now make your way ahead, parallel to the fence (and easier walking some ten metres from it) to reach the small gate and stile on your right at the crest of the hill. Warning: In mist or fog do not lose sight of the fence.*
7. *Turn right and go over the stile, then straight ahead over two more stiles. Just before a pylon cross a stile to the field on your right but continue in the same direction over another stile at the next fence.*
8. *Bear slightly right to continue along the bluff. At the end of the crags follow the stone wall.*
9. *Just beyond a diagonal sign cross a stile/fence ahead. Continue slightly right for about 200 metres to meet the boundary wall above the house.*
10. *Cut off the right-hand corner of the wall to soon find a stile leading you onto the driveway. At the road turn right and head down towards the City Arms.*
11. *Retrace your steps to Minera.*

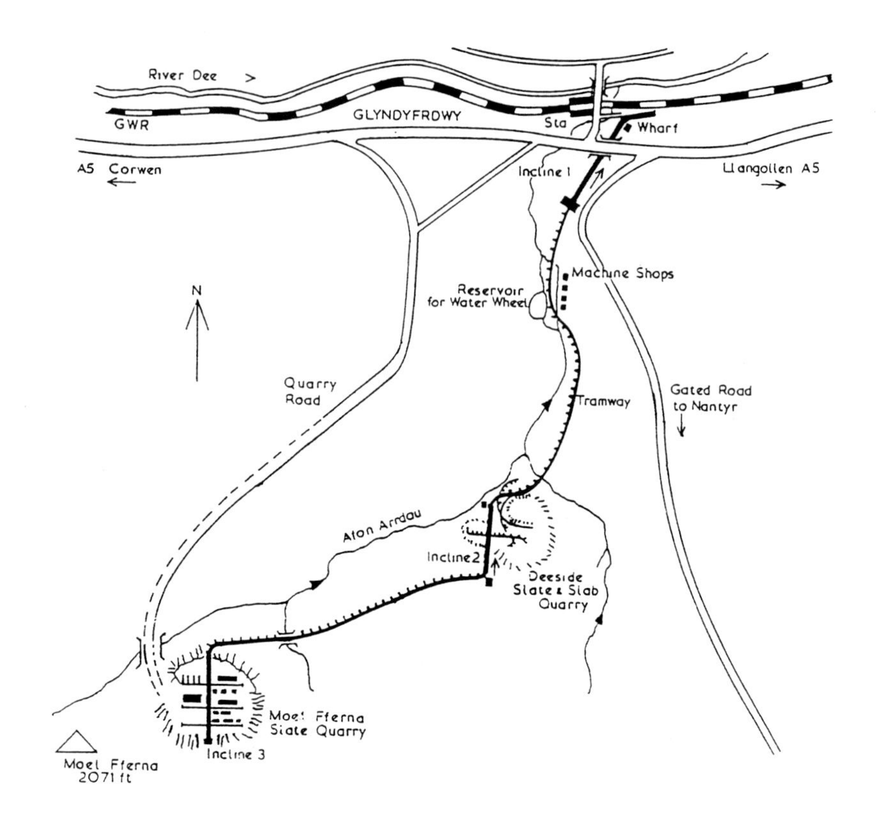

THE SLATE QUARRIES: INDUSTRIAL ARCHAEOLOGY

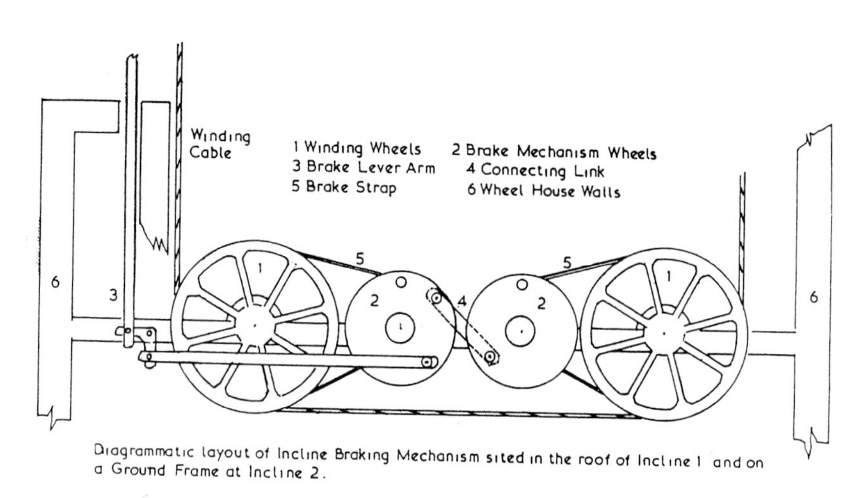

Diagrammatic layout of Incline Braking Mechanism sited in the roof of Incline 1 and on a Ground Frame at Incline 2.

Route 10 **2 miles**

The old slate works

Outline Glyndyfrdwy — slate works — reservoir — mountain road — tramway incline — Glyndyfrdwy.

Summary Climb steadily up the wooded valley on a slightly muddy path and descend along a lane then down steps.

Attractions Not only are there the natural attractions of woodland, waterfalls and views on this delightful short walk, but also you can see some interesting industrial remains.

A large waterwheel-housing and some sheds are all that remain of the slate works at the first site you reach. This was the dressing floor for both the Moel Fferna Slate Mine and the Deeside Slab Quarry. During the 19th and early 20th centuries the mine (near the Moel Fferna summit) and the quarry (a mile below the summit) produced large slabs of slate from the Ludlow and Wenlock Shales present here in the Berwyn Mountains. The slabs were sent down a tramway to the workshops. They were then planed and cut to size using machinery and saws driven by water-power. The resulting slates were known by such names as Duchesses, Marchionesses, Countesses, Viscountesses, Ladies, Small Ladies, Doubles and Randoms, depending on their size. Other items produced included slabs for tombs, headstones, flagstones and chimney-pieces.

Each team of six men, known as a 'bargain', consisted of quarrymen, splitters and dressers. In the quarry each bargain worked a horizontal stretch of 10 yards with a 15 yard vertical face. This was let to the bargain by the quarry company and in return the finished slate was bought from the men by the company. A bargain produced about 35 tons of finished slate in a week. In 1877 the price paid for this would have been under 7 shillings (35p) a ton. After paying rent, wages for the manager, clerks and 'trammers', as well as tools and other overheads, the company would make a clear profit of about twice this amount.

Above the work area are the remains of the unique 'wooden tramway'. Originally this consisted of 7ft 6in long 6ft × 4in rails joined by iron fish-plates and separated by iron rods at regular intervals. The rails were shod with iron strips and the whole tramway was embedded in the ground.

Eventually, the quarry was served by a road and the tramway was left to rot. The iron strips on the rails were removed for the war effort (World War Two). The quarry finally closed in 1947 and the entrances to the mine were sealed by blasting.

continued on page 47

Route 10

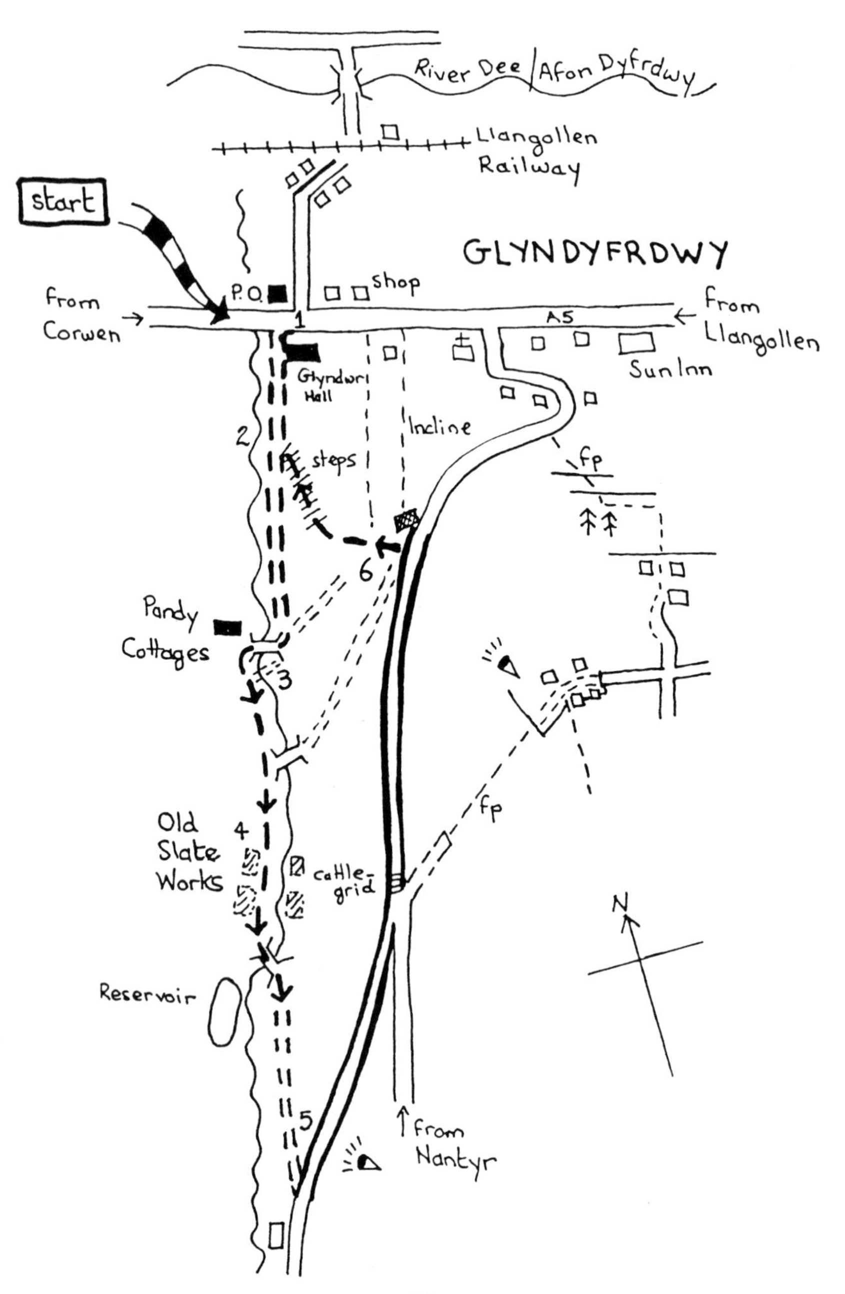

River Dee
Afon Dyfrdwy
Llangollen
Railway
start
GLYNDYFRDWY
P.O.
shop
from
Corwen
A5
from
Llangollen
1
Glyndwr
Hall
Sun Inn
2
steps
Incline
fp
6
Pandy
Cottages
3
fp
Old
Slate
Works
4
cattle-
grid
N
Reservoir
5
from
Nantyr

Route 10

The old slate works — 2 miles

START: *Glyndyfrdwy Post Office on the A5 west of Llangollen. G.R. SJ 149427. Buses from Wrexham, Llangollen & Bala. Trains from Llangollen (from Glyndyfrdwy Station go south through the village and climb the hill to the A5).*

ROUTE

1. *From the post office, cross the main road and take the track beside the Glyndwr Hall.*
2. *Follow this track uphill, ignoring steps and track to your left.*
3. *Cross the stream over the small bridge by a ford. Continue upstream past 'Pandy Cottages' and waterfalls.*
4. *You soon reach the ruined workings. From here follow the tramway in its deep cutting as it crosses a slab bridge beside a disused reservoir. Continue upstream.*
5. *At the lane turn sharp left. When you meet the mountain road beside a cattle-grid, turn left again.*
6. *At the corner of the road (at the hut after the tramway bed joins from the left but before the steep incline to the railway) turn left. Find the steps beyond the head of the incline and descend to rejoin your outward route. Retrace your steps to the Post Office.*

As you follow the footpath you will see the slab bridge for the tramway and the reservoir for the water-wheel. On the way back look for a shed at the top of the incline leading down to the railway at Glyndyfrdwy. This contained the braking mechanism for the trucks.

Refreshments The Sun Inn on the A5 at Glyndyfrdwy serves meals. There is a village store at the start of the walk.

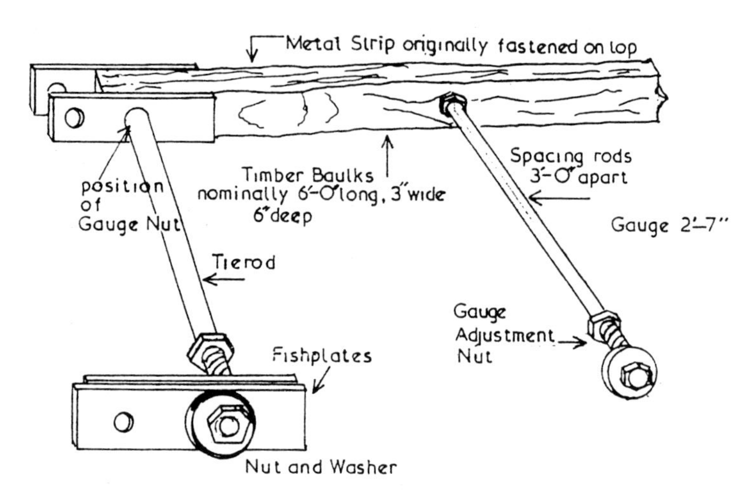

Details of Tramway to Moel Fferna Slate Quarry as observed 31-5-1971

CONTEMPLATION

Route 11 **3 miles**

Chirk Castle and Aqueduct

Outline Station — Castle Gates — Pont Faen — Chirk Bank — Chirk Aqueduct — Canal Tunnel — Station.

Summary This walk can be combined with a visit to the castle in summer (see the appendices for details of opening times) but note that the castle drive is a mile long and that it might be worth a separate day's visit if you want to see the interior and wander around the gardens as well.

The magnificient castle gates are passed on the route, which then uses the 17th century Chester-to-Cardiff road, now just a path, to reach the River Ceiriog. After a stroll through the waterside meadows you climb a short section of road to the canal towpath and cross the viaduct to go through the tunnel. Although there is a handrail in the tunnel, it is recommended that you keep dogs on a lead. You may also like to take a torch with you. An alternative route that avoids the tunnel is given.

Attractions The castle gates date from the early 18th century although they were moved to occupy their present position after the railway was built. See if you can pick out all the different motifs in the ironwork. The 'hand' at the top is from the family shield of the Myddletons who have inhabited the castle for about 500 years.

Chirk Castle was one of Edward I's fortifications; one of the few that were not served by sea. The main defences were built at the end of the 13th century but towers and curtain walls have been altered and rebuilt over the centuries. If you visit the castle you will find treasures presented to Sir Richard Myddleton from Sir Francis Drake, and can peer into the deep dungeon. In legend the curse of 'the hand' upon the Myddleton family can only be removed if a prisoner survives 10 years in this dismal cell.

Chirk Aqueduct and the higher railway viaduct that tower above you as you follow the course of the River Ceiriog, were built in the 18th and 19th centuries respectively. The aqueduct is now a tourist attraction, especially for boaters who hire narrowboats for their journey to Llangollen. When the aqueduct was built however, the canal was a lifeline to the people in the Welsh valleys who wanted to export raw materials from their mines and quarries to the cities and towns of England. Occasionally you will see one of the original trading boats that were pulled by horse-power. These have become collectors' items and show off their traditional back cabins, brasswork, and pictures of roses and castles which give the canals their colourful traditions. Books on the canal and cut-out models of traditional

continued on page 51

Route 11

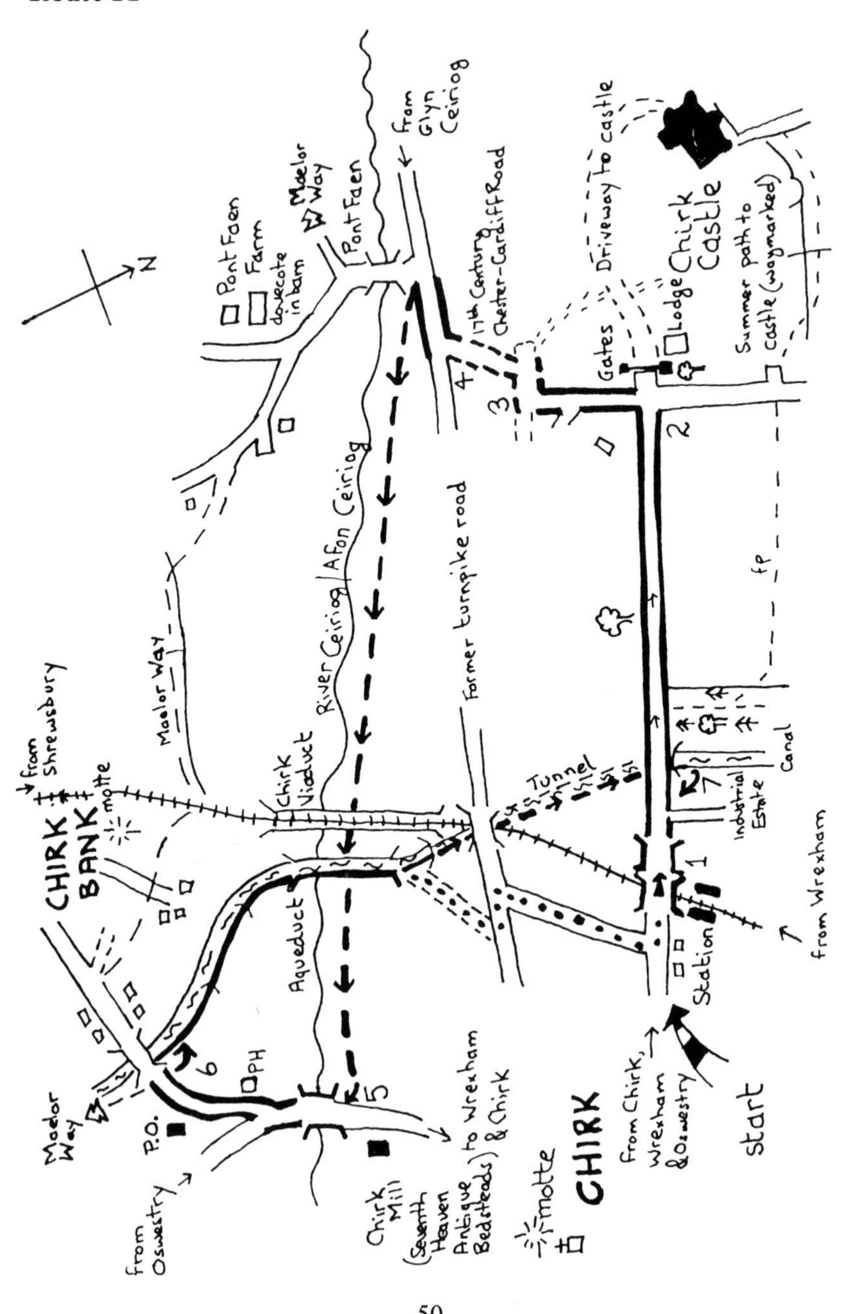

N
Pont Faen Farm
dovecote in barn
Maelor Way
Pont Faen
from Glyn Ceiriog
Driveway to castle
17th Century Chester-Cardiff Road
Chirk Castle
Lodge
Gates
Summer path to castle (waymarked)
River Ceiriog / Afon Ceiriog
Former turnpike road
fp
from Shrewsbury
CHIRK BANK
motte
Maelor Way
Chirk Viaduct
Tunnel
Canal
Industrial Estate
Aqueduct
from Wrexham
Station
PH
P.O.
Maelor Way
from Oswestry
to Wrexham & Chirk
Chirk Mill (Seventh Heaven Antique Bedsteads)
motte
CHIRK
From Chirk, Wrexham & Oswestry
Start
1
2
3
4
5
6
7

Route 11

Chirk Castle and Aqueduct 3 miles

START: *Chirk Station G.R. SJ 284377. The station is on the Chester–Shrewsbury line. Cars can be parked on lanes nearby. The regular Wrexham–Oswestry buses serve the village with occasional buses from Llangollen.*

Alternatives *Those who do not like heights can return by the outward route from Chirk Bank. To avoid only the tunnel, cross the aqueduct then climb to the road above. Turn left, then right to the station.*

ROUTE

1. *From the station cross the bridge over the railway and follow the road to the prominent castle gates.*
2. *Unless you wish to visit the castle first, turn left and follow the lane, then the path ahead, beside the caravan site.*
3. *At the T-junction turn right and immediately left down the footpath (once the main Chester-Cardiff road).*
4. *At the next road turn right to Pont Faen, a stone bridge across the Afon Ceiriog. Take the riverside path to your left, passing under the viaduct and aqueduct continuing to the road.*
5. *Turn right opposite Chirk Mill (now Seventh Heaven Antique Beds, open to browsers) then fork right, uphill.*
6. *When you reach the canal turn right along the towpath to cross the aqueduct and go through the tunnel.*
7. *Turn sharp right up the slope, then turn left at the road to the station.*

---

narrowboats are available from the Chirk Bank Post Office, which you pass.

Refreshments There are two cafés in Chirk village as well as 'The Hand Inn' which serves varied refreshment throughout the day. On the walk, the post office sells soft drinks, ice-lollies etc.

MOUNTAIN GATE

Refreshments The New Inn (0978 840471) serves a variety of moderately priced meals (lunchtime and evening) and caters for vegetarians and vegans.

On a hot summer day there is no better place for a picnic than the cool summit of Ruabon Mountain but please take your litter (and anyone else's you find) home with you.

Route 12 **3 or 6 miles**

Ruabon Mountain

Outline Rhosllanerchrugog — Ty Canol — Ruabon Mountain — Tainant — Rhosllanerchrugog.

Summary As you climb gradually, but continuously from the large village of Rhosllanerchrugog (Rhos) you cannot help but see the bulk of Ruabon Mountain ahead. Although a mile of the route is along a country lane, this is little used by traffic and has five separate seats along the way. Nevertheless, keep your children on the right-hand side facing oncoming traffic and walk a little in front of them to warn any approaching vehicles.

As you climb, the view opens out until you reach the summit, where, on a clear day, a panorama unfolds over Wrexham and the plains of Cheshire and Shropshire.

You are warned not to leave the mountain path without map and compass.

The return is over fields and down lanes to the village. A short alternative is to park at the mountain gate (SJ 264473) and follow the path to the summit. This part of the route descends the same way so you can shorten your walk at any time by turning back to the lane.

Attractions Look for a variety of roadside and hedgerow plants throughout the seasons as you follow the lane which, as one writer put it 'has been used by Rhosites for generations'.

I wonder how many thousands of years people have been trekking over the mountain? Beside the moorland path are the remaining hollow-ways which became disused after years of erosion and have now become recolonised with heather and reed. See if you can spot the three varieties of heather here: ling, cross-leaved heath, and bell heather—the names of two of them give clues to their identities.

Although the views are clearer on fine days in winter and spring perhaps late summer is the best time to walk this route as you can then munch blackberries on the way up the lane and revert to bilberries (whinberries) on the mountain.

The cross on the summit is 'in memoriam' to two pilots who died in an aeroplane crash here during World War Two—one of at least fifteen allied aircraft that crashed on this mountain. Wreckage from planes still turns up—often along with unexploded bombs: an estimated 500 or so were dropped on this mountain during 1940 when decoy lights were set up to fool 'the enemy' into believing that this was Liverpool.

continued opposite

Route 12

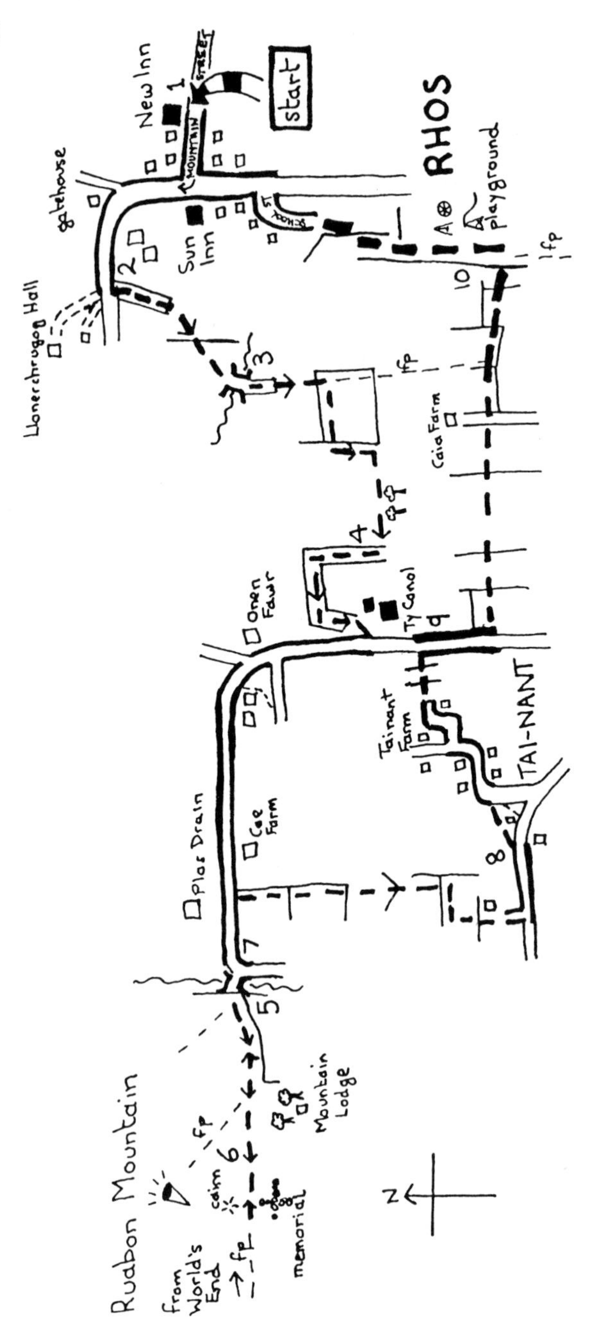

start
New Inn
1
Mountain Street
RHOS
playground
fp
10
Sun Inn
School St
gatehouse
2
Llanerchrugog Hall
3
fp
Caia Farm
4
Onen Fawr
Ty Canol
9
Tainant Farm
TAI-NANT
8
Cae Farm
Plas Drain
7
5
Ruabon Mountain
Mountain Lodge
fp
6
cairn
memorial
From World's End
fp
N

Route 12

Ruabon Mountain 3 or 6 miles

START: *Y Dafarn Newydd/The New Inn, Mountain Street, Rhosllanerchrugog (Rhos) near Wrexham G.R. SJ 292468. Buses go to Rhos from Wrexham. The inn has a car park for patrons.*

Alternative *For the short walk park near the mountain gate at G.R. SJ 264473 and follow directions 5 & 6.*

ROUTE

1. *Face the door of the inn and turn left along Mountain Street. At the T-junction, opposite the Sun Inn, turn right and follow the road.*
2. *In 500 metres take the enclosed path on your left opposite two driveways. At the end turn half-right; cross the next stile and continue in the same direction.*
3. *After the bridge and another enclosed path, turn right to cross a stile at the top of the field before turning left, then right to go up the line of trees that marks the former field boundary.*
4. *Skirt right around the buildings to reach the lane. Turn right, and ignore left and right turns. In a mile, when you reach the dip and the sharp left-hand corner, go ahead onto the mountain.*
5. *Follow the main track slightly left, which at first follows the boundary and then goes straight to the summit, marked by a cairn and a cross of stones.*
6. *Return to the lane by the same path.*
7. *Retrace your steps 500 metres along the lane, then turn right onto the footpath. Go straight ahead across 4 fields. (The latter 2 are cut diagonally.) Use the gate and track down to a stile at the rear of a house, then follow the drive to the lane and turn left.*
8. *In 60 metres fork left. (There is an alternative beyond the next house if the hedges are still uncut.) Follow the lane ahead then turn right down the 'no through road'. At the end follow the path directly ahead using 2 gates and 3 iron stiles to reach the next lane.*
9. *Ty Canol is to your left but turn right and take the first path on your left, which heads more or less straight down 5 fields, across a track and down another 4 fields to the children's playground in the village of Rhos.*
10. *Turn left along the track and, beyond the corner, use one of the stiles on your right to continue along beside the track into 'School Street'. At the T-junction turn left to the Sun Inn then right to the New Inn.*

HOUSE IN MARFORD

Route 13 **3 miles**

Marford Quarry

Outline Trevor Arms Hotel — Marford Quarry — Turnpike road — Trevor Arms.

Summary From the hotel you follow a lane to Marford Quarry where you may either explore the maze of paths yourself, or follow the suggested route. The route continues through woodland to the top of the hill and then descends by a footpath behind the quarry.

Attractions This lower part of the village of Marford was once owned by the Trevalyn Estate. It was they who, in the early 19th century, had the Gothic cottages constructed, although many were alterations from earlier houses dating from the 17th century.

The Trevor Arms was once a coaching inn and the road in front went straight up the hill beside it. The final path in this walk will bring you down the remains of that road which probably dates from Norman times, and which later became a turnpike road. As a public highway for so many years it is difficult to believe how anyone ever managed to fence a part of it off and claim it as their own. Quarrying operations destroyed the remains of a Norman motte and bailey castle which once guarded the road and looked out over the plain toward England.

Marford Quarry was recently purchased by the North Wales Wildlife Trust and is now open to the public as a Nature Reserve. (See the appendix for the address of the Trust which has other reserves in the area.)

On the route look out for:
The Trevor Coat of Arms
Gothic cottages
A gargoyle
A cat on a roof
The sign of an owl
A fence made from railway lines
Unusual wild flowers (not to be picked for any reason)
Colourful dragonflies
Spotted butterflies
Squirrels
A view to the Peckforton Hill
A view of Jodrell Bank Radio Telescope (in front of the hills)
The old turnpike road

When you reach the lane above the quarry, the first bungalow on your

continued on page 59

Route 13

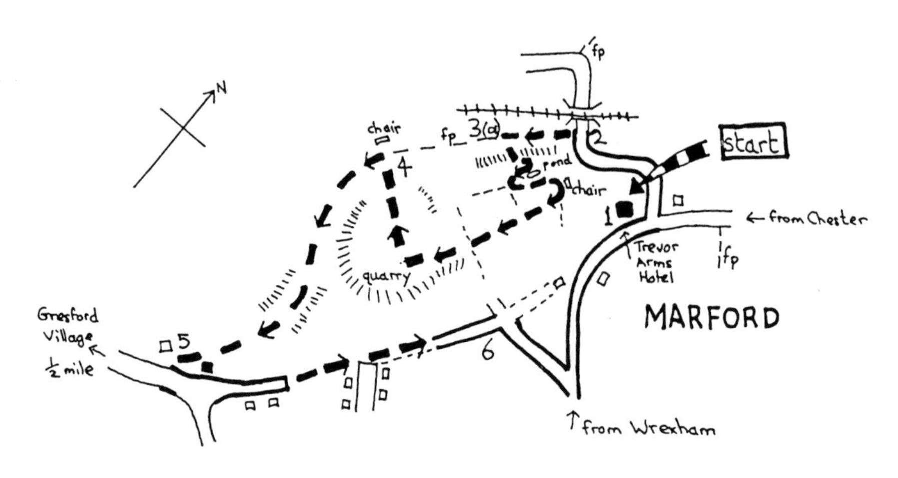

CANADA GOOSE black, brown, white 100cm

Route 13

Marford Quarry — 3 miles

START: *Trevor Arms Hotel, Marford G.R. SJ 359562. Buses from Wrexham and Chester. Parking in the Hotel car park by request at reception.*

ROUTE

1. *From the car park turn left, then left along the lane.*
2. *Before the railway bridge fork left into Marford Quarry.*
3. *EITHER explore the maze of paths in the quarry at will, returning to continue along the main footpath, OR*

3a. *Follow the suggested route: fork sharp left up the stony path, pass the pond, turn left and left again to the small open area with a seat. Turn right, then fork right and cross a number of paths to head for the high slopes—passing below the slopes into the central open area. Turn right to find a seat on the main footpath. Turn left.*

4. *Ignore right forks and continue along the footpath, marked by the remains of a fence which used railway sleepers and lines as posts.*
5. *Beyond the wood, at the road, turn left and immediately fork left. At the end of the short road go down the enclosed path and continue on to another.*
6. *Follow the lane ahead, turning right at the junction and left at the main road, using the pavement to reach the Trevor Arms Hotel.*

---

left is the home of the Ramblers' Welsh Officer—call in for more information, a programme of walks and a membership application form (office hours only).

Refreshments As well as having an outdoor childrens's play area, the Trevor Arms Hotel serves a variety of meals and caters for vegetarians.

CHAPEL AT OVERTON

Route 14 **2 miles**

Llan-y-cefn Wood

Outline Overton Church — Almshouses — Pendyffryn Wood — River Dee — Llan-y-cefn Wood — Llan-y-cefn — 'The Bottoms' — Overton Church.

Summary A fairly flat walk except for the short drop down from the village and the short climb back up later on. The walk may be muddy after wet weather.

Attractions Five of the so-called 'Seven Wonders of Wales' are in the Borderlands. This church in the ancient village of Overton is famous for its yew trees:

Pistyll Rhaedr and Wrexham steeple
Snowdons's mountain without its people,
Overton yew trees, St. Winefride's Wells
Llangollen Bridge, and Gresford bells

The flesh of the red yew berries looks delicious and succulent in autumn and it is, but THE SEED WITHIN IS DEADLY POISONOUS so take care with very young children.

Look out for some of the interesting buildings in the village:

the Rectory
the Bryn-y-Pys Estate Office of the early 18th century.
the 'Cocoa and Reading Rooms', built by the local Lord-of-the-manor to try to encourage sobriety here, is now the local library.
the almshouses, built in 1848
the small chapel on the return journey
the 'Gothic cottages' at the end of the route.

Llan-y-cefn (church ridge) takes its name from the church at Erbistock built on a rectory site dating from the 13th century. Next to the church is the Boat Inn. Unfortunately the small ferry, which carried 10,000 passengers a year over into the woods or vice-versa, ceased operation in 1939. The winch still remains on the other side of the river. The old ford alongside is nearly 3 feet deep in summer but was regularly used by soldiers in World War Two.

Llan-y-cefn Wood, and the two fields within, are alive with wildlife throughout the year. In spring and summer carry a field guide to recognise plants such as monkey-flower and kingcup, dog's-mercury and wood anemone, yellow archangel and woodruff.

Late spring also brings the orange-tip butterfly, followed by a variety of colourful butterflies and dragonflies throughout the summer.

continued on page 64

Route 14

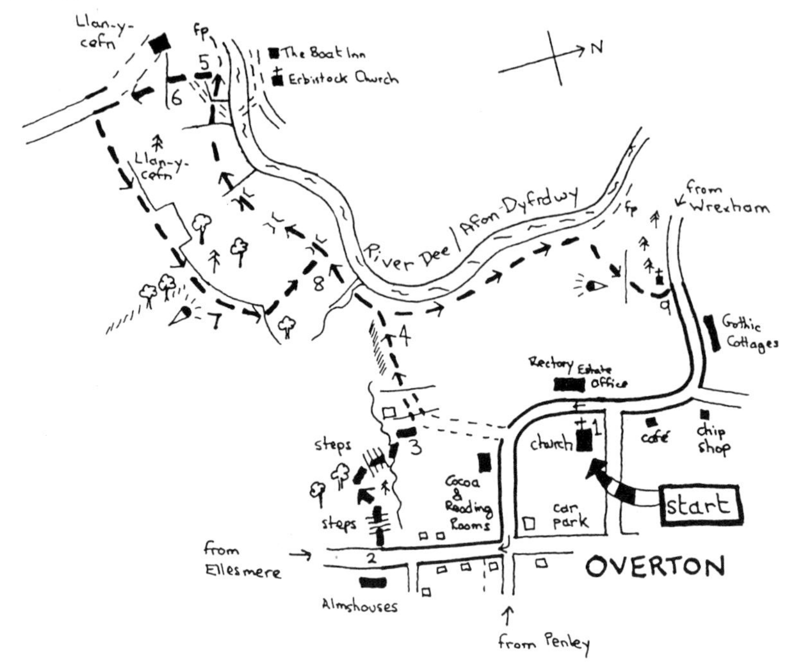

HORSESHOE FALLS (Route 1)

Route 14

Llan-y-cefn Wood 2 miles

START: *Overton-on-Dee Church G.R. SJ 374418. Buses run from Wrexham (infrequent, check times). The village car park is behind the church.*

ROUTE

1. *Facing out of the church turn left. Around the corner, at the crossroad, turn right.*
2. *Past 'Springfield Park' and, opposite some old almshouses, follow the signposted path down through Pendyffryn Wood. Cross the streams and continue behind the high fence.*
3. *At the track turn left. Cross stiles beside gates to enter the large field and follow the embankment path slightly left to the river.*
4. *Turn left and soon follow the main path through Llan-y-cefn wood. Beyond the fields, after you re-enter the woodland, you reach the ferry steps opposite the Boat Inn and Erbistock Church.*
5. *Turn left up the bank. Cross the next field keeping the house to your right as you approach the far boundary.*
6. *Take the narrow path uphill to the driveway and continue ahead. Take the first small bridlegate on your left and follow the field boundary on your left.*
7. *Beyond an embankment find a stile on your left in the bottom corner of the field. Head straight down to rejoin the main path in Llan-y-cefn Wood.*
8. *Turn right and retrace your steps through the wood towards Overton, but continue along the river bank 800 metres or so past the outward path junction. Turn right and find the clear path heading up through the trees.*
9. *Past the small chapel, at the road, turn right and continue to Overton.*

Budding ornithologists should bring binoculars to catch a glimpse of the occasional kingfisher or cormorant. Wagtail, mallard and moorhen are more common on the river and treecreeper, jay and woodpecker might be seen or heard in the wood—the jay living up to its Welsh name sgrech-y-coed (screecher of the wood).

Refreshments Metcalfes of Overton, in the main street, have a coffee-shop which serves tasty homemade meals, including vegetarian dishes. The cafe is closed on Mondays and Thursdays. There is also a chip shop and there are several village stores. Opposite the Boat Inn is a wooden seat, ideal for a picnic and those who feel like a swim, or have kitted themselves out with waders, can go over to the inn for a pint.

CANAL BASIN

Route 15 **2, 4 or 6 miles**

Three Meres

Outline Canal Wharf — Ellesmere Tunnel — Blake Mere — Cole Mere — Blake Mere — Ellesmere Tunnel — The Mere — Canal Wharf.

Summary A flat walk along the beautiful Llangollen Canal with two shorter alternatives which miss out one of the meres.

Attractions Beside the Canal Wharf stand the warehouses signwritten with the 19th century name of the canal company: Shropshire Union Railways and Canal Company.

The canal, with its arm to Ellesmere, was planned in 1791 to link the rivers Mersey, Severn and Dee. Due to financial problems and competition from another canal to Shrewsbury, the original plan was never completed. The canal which passes Ellesmere, known today as the Llangollen Canal, was only intended to reach the town as a branch of the main line (which was to be cut several miles to the east). It ended up being extended past Ellesmere as the main line connecting with the Chester Canal.

Thomas Telford was the 'General Agent', Surveyor, Engineer, Architect and Overlooker of the Works' for the Ellesmere canal and soon replaced his superior, William Jessop, as Chief Engineer.

After the waterway was linked to the Chester Canal the two canal companies became one. A later amalgamation was made with the Birmingham and Liverpool Junction Canal and then in 1846 several interests joined to form the Shropshire Union Railways and Canal Company. A lease to the London and North Western Railway kept the canal open into the railway age, as LNWR competed for trade with their rival Great Western Railways who ran the trains on the border. Nowadays British Waterways Board control the canal.

There is more canal architecture on the walk: buildings at the canal junction, Ellesmere Tunnel, a sluice and the (stone) EC and (metal) SUC boundary markers on the path around Cole Mere.

Take binoculars to see some of the water birds on the meres: little and crested grebes are resident, black-throated divers are winter visitors and can often be seen on Black Mere, tufted ducks and mallard are common here as are the Canada geese and coots who approach for food. For the last two years, during the herons' nesting season between March and June, the RSPB have supplied a Heron Watch with telescopes on the shore of The Mere.

Refreshments There are cafes, pubs, take-aways and chip shops in the town. At Cole Mere Country Park, halfway around the route, there are toilets and picnic tables.

Route 15

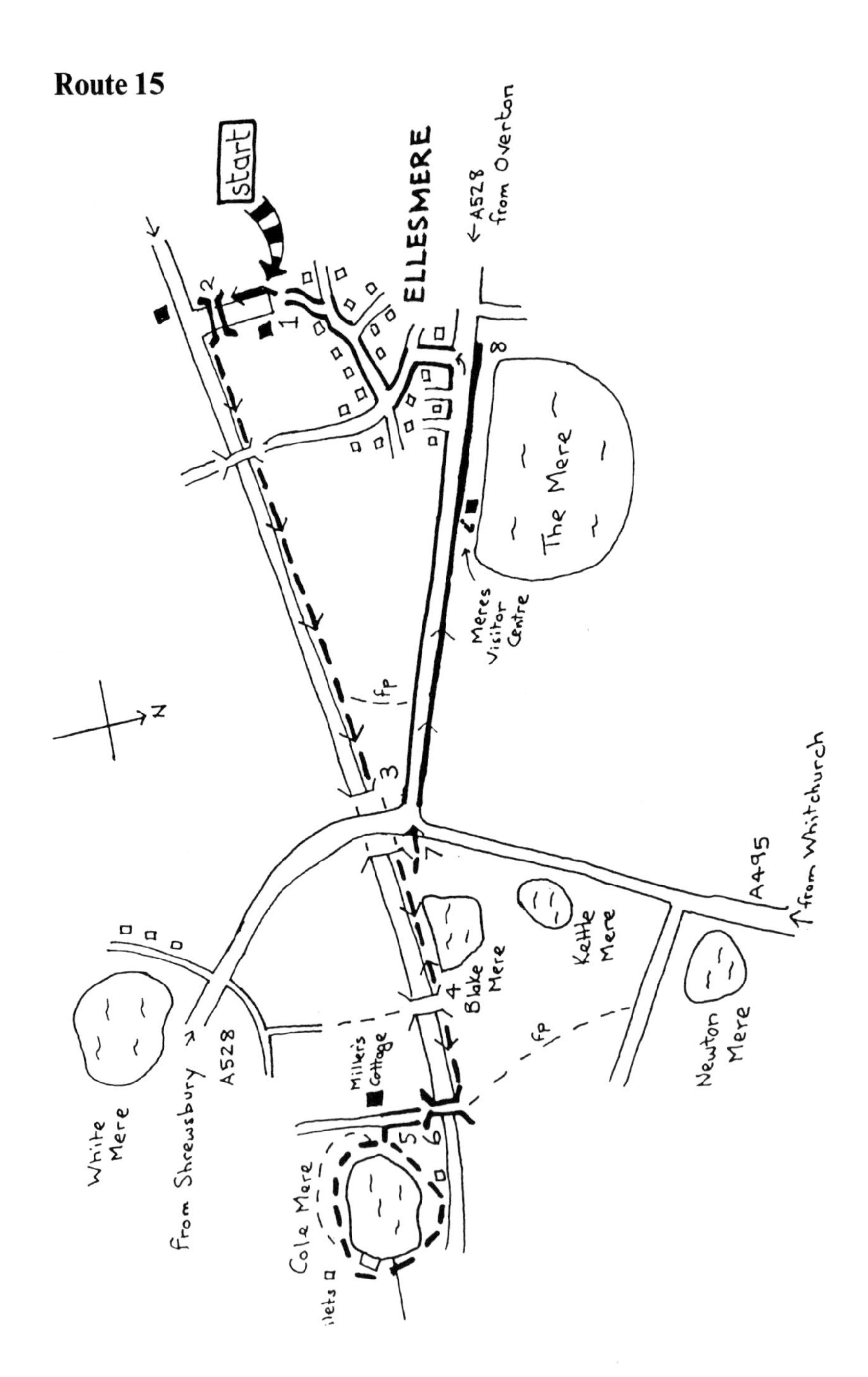
start
ELLESMERE
← A528 from Overton
The Mere
Meres Visitor Centre
fp
N
A495
↑ from Whitchurch
Kettle Mere
Blake Mere
Newton Mere
Millers Cottage
White Mere
from Shrewsbury ↗
A528
Cole Mere
1
2
3
4
5
6
7
8

Route 15

Three Meres — 2, 4 or 6 miles

START: *Ellesmere Canal Wharf (well-signposted) G.R. SJ 398346. Buses to Ellesmere from Oswestry link with the Chester–Shrewsbury train line at Gobowen station. There are also buses from Wrexham. Parking space is usually available by the wharf.*

Alternatives *For the shortest route follow directions 1–3, continue along the towpath to Blake Mere then return to the tunnel and follow directions 7–8. For the 4 mile route miss out direction 5.*

ROUTE:

1. *Facing the canal wharf follow the towpath on your right.*
2. *At the canal junction turn left and go over White Bridge.*
3. *Continue along the towpath for half a mile and go through the tunnel. Keep children and dogs under strict control in the tunnel.*
4. *From the next bridge there is a path, right, to the road near White Mere but your route continues along the towpath and crosses the next bridge by the thatched 'Miller's Cottage'. In 50 metres turn left onto the shore of Cole Mere.*
5. *Go either way around the mere and return to this point.*
6. *Return over the bridge and along the canal past Blake Mere.*
7. *Take the path up beside the tunnel entrance. Cross the road via the island, and head along the pavement for Ellesmere.*
8. *Beyond The Mere follow signs to Canal Wharf, turning left into Watergate Street, right into High Street, left into Cross Street and left into Wharf Road.*

CAERGWRLE CASTLE

Route 16 ½, 2½ or 5 miles

Caergwrle Castle and Hope Mountain

Outline Caergwrle — Castle — Caergwrle — Bryn Yorkin — Waun-y-llyn Country Park — Hope Mountain — Bryn Yorkin — Caergwrle.

Summary This could actually be split into two walks, one to the castle and another on to Hope Mountain. There are a few scrambles in the woods at Bryn Yorkin and the total ascent is nearly 1200 feet. Young children may find this walk difficult—for them just the ascent to the castle would be enough.

Attractions The ruin of Caergwrle Castle is surrounded by a defensive embankment from an earlier period. The stone castle dates from 1278 when Edward I gave Dafydd 100 marks 'for the building of his castle at Kaierguill'. Dafydd had fought for the English against his half-brother Llewelyn who was later exiled to Snowdonia.

Once the castle was built Dafydd changed sides and attacked Hawarden Castle. Llewelyn reluctantly joined the fray which ended when an English footsoldier killed him with a spear. Dafydd, unloved by Welsh and English alike, was handed over by the Welsh and hanged for treason by the English.

The King's forces had arrived at the castle to find it dismantled but within a few months it was rebuilt by 30 masons and 340 carpenters employed by the Crown. The following year Edward presented the building to his queen but, later, it burnt down. Despite later conditions in a grant of Edward II to a John de Cromwell, that the castle was to be repaired, no work seems to have been done.

See if you can find the early embankments, the moat, and the different stonework in the upper walls. Look too for the large internal oven, the 'waste disposal chutes' in the stonework under the ivy, the base of the largest round tower ever built in a Welsh Castle, and the mill wheel (below the tower base) cut from the bedrock in the 18th century.

The main walk visits Waun-y-Llyn Country Park where you can wander at leisure around the gorse and heather moorland. However, when you reach the lane at the top of the hill you can choose the shortcut instead: down through the woods on Bryn Yorkin, and beside the stone manor house of the same name, back to Caergwrle.

Refreshments Take a picnic to the castle or Waun-y-llyn Country Park. Alternatively visit the Old Castle Inn, or the Bridge Inn below the station. Both inns serve hot meals, including vegetarian dishes.

Route 16

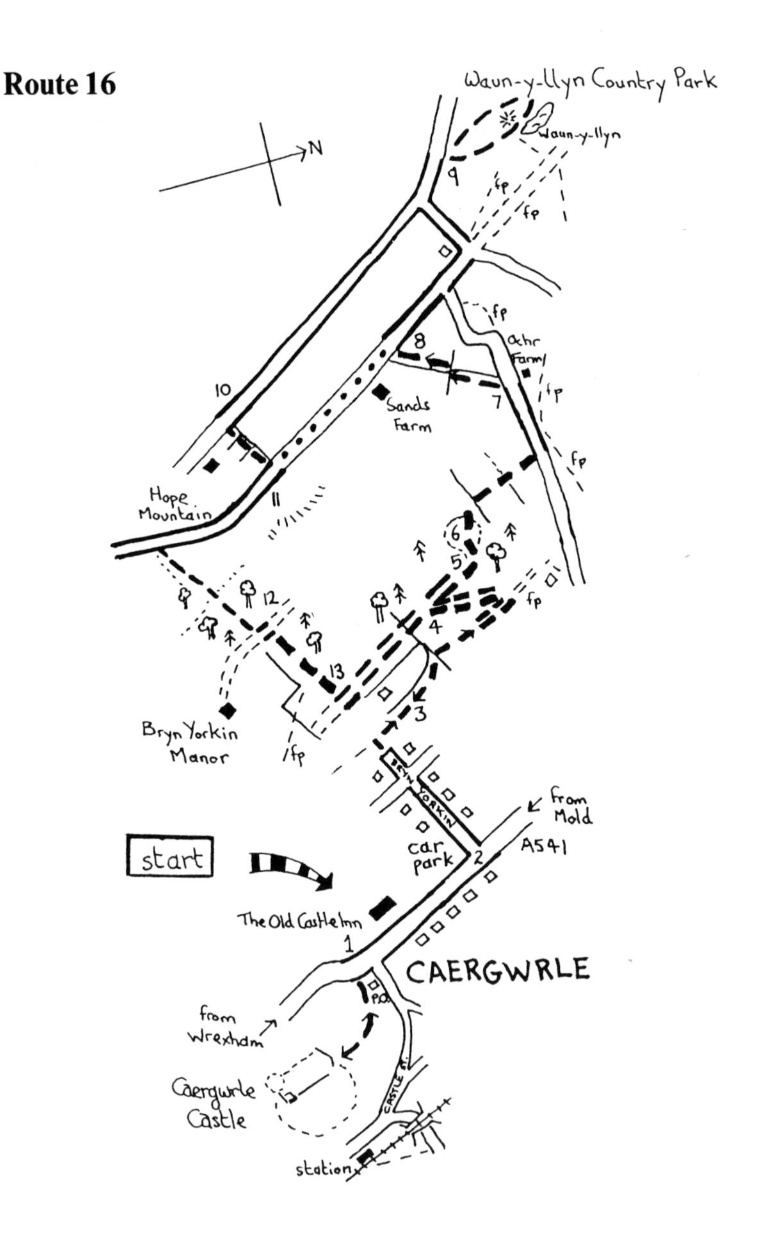

partly-stone stile. Descend by the wall, later ignoring a stile on the right.

13. *At the next track turn left. After the stile fork right then turn sharp right at the lower track to retrace your steps back to the village.*

Route 16

Caergwrle Castle and Hope Mountain — ½, 2 or 5 miles

START: *The Old Castle Inn, Caergwrle. G.R. SJ 306574. Buses from Wrexham and Mold. Trains on the Wrexham–Bidston line (from the station entrance turn right then left to the village). Car park in the village.*

Alternatives *For the shortest walk follow direction 1 only. For the 2 mile walk follow 2–7, turn left past Sands Farm then follow 11–13.*

ROUTE:

1. *Follow the steps beside the post office to the castle, return the same way.*
2. *Take 'Bryn Yorkin' beside the car park, uphill to its end. Follow the path ahead then turn right.*
3. *Ignore 2 stiles on the left but go ahead over another. Fork sharp left up the track.*
4. *Fork sharp right at the next track.*
5. *At junctions stay on the main path, a hollow way once used as a tram line: tram rails assure you that you are going the right way.*
6. *In the quarry, by the tramway junction, bear right and continue along the bank. Take the stile on your right and descend ahead down the rough path with a few scrambles. At the lane turn left. (A right turn here leads back to the village.)*
7. *Over the first brow of the hill, opposite 'Ochr Farm', cross the well-hidden stile up in the embankment on your left. Follow boundary on your right, go through the first gate, then follow the boundary on your left to the lane. (The shortcut can be taken from here.)*
8. *Turn right, ignore the lane down to the right, then at the T-junction follow the signs to the Country Park (left then right).*
9. *After wandering at will return to the entrance and turn left. Take the first lane right.*
10. *In 800 metres (50 metres after the power lines) take the stile on your left. Beyond the next stile take the gate ahead and follow the boundary on your left. At the lane turn right.*
11. *(The shortcut continues from here.) In over 500 metres, after ignoring a stile and gate on the left, take the stile on your left. Head 20° left to find the path descending from the woodland boundary by the rowan tree.*
12. *When this reaches a track turn left and immediately right beyond the*

continued opposite

APPENDICES

ROUTES IN ORDER OF DIFFICULTY Easy–Hard

Route 16 — *½ mile*
Route 5 — *¾ mile*
Route 1 — *1½ miles*
Route 7 — *1 mile*
Route 15 — *2 miles*
Route 8 — *2 miles*
Route 5 — *2 miles*
Route 14 — *2 miles*
Route 7 — *3 miles*
Route 3 — *3 miles*
Route 8 — *3 miles*
Route 13 — *3 miles*
Route 15 — *4 miles*
Route 11 — *3 miles*
Route 6 — *3½ miles*
Route 5 — *4 miles*
Route 6 — *4 miles*
Route 10 — *2 miles*
Route 2 — *3 miles*
Route 1 — *4 miles*
Route 12 — *3 miles*
Route 15 — *6 miles*
Route 16 — *2½ miles*
Route 3 — *4 miles*
Route 4 — *4 miles*
Route 9 — *3 miles*
Route 16 — *5 miles*
Route 12 — *6 miles*

PUBLIC TRANSPORT

Remember to check return times before you start.

Trains

British Rail Chester 0244 340170

Buses

Crosville Wales Wrexham 0978 261361
Wrights of Wrexham 0978 265327

TOURIST INFORMATION OFFICES

Wrexham Guildhall—0978 357845
Llangollen Town Hall—0978 860828
Whitchurch Civic Centre—0948 4577
Chester Town Hall—0244 313126
Chester Visitor Centre—0244 318916/351609
Ellesmere 'Meres Visitor Centre'—0691 622981
Oswestry Mile End Services, A5—0691 662488
Oswestry Library—0691 662753

WHERE TO GO AND WHAT TO SEE

Chester, Cheshire

There are lots of indoor things to do in the city and some easy walks, for example: around the walls, along the canal towpath, around the Roodee (Chester racecourse), and across The Meadows by the River Dee. If you want some planned walks try the set of reasonably priced 'Tourcards' giving 'Six Circular Walks around Chester'. Alternatively follow a guided 'Roman Soldier Wall Patrol', 'Ghosthunter Trail' or 'Pastfinder Tour' from the Information Office at the Town Hall. Short boat trips start from the Groves, beside the River Dee.

Toy Museum, 13a Lower Bridge Street. *Includes the largest matchbox toy collection in the world.* 7 days 11am–5pm. Admission Charge. 0244 346297.

Chester Heritage Centre, Bridge Street. *The history of Chester in sound and picture.* Mon–Sat 11am–7pm, Sun 12pm–5pm. Admission charge to non-residents. 0244 317948.

Grosvenor Museum, Grosvenor Road. *Period rooms, Roman history, exhibitions, video, shop.* Amost all year, Mon–Sat 10.30am–5pm, Sun 2pm–5pm. Free admission.

Military Museum, Grosvenor Road. *Artefacts, uniforms and regimentation of 4 regiments from C17th.* Daily 9am–5pm, not Good Friday, closed over Christmas.

Chester Visitor Centre, 2 Vicars Lane. *Videos, crafts, Victorian Street, cafe, bookshop.* 7 days, long hours. Free admission. 0244 318916.

Water Tower, NW corner of city walls. *Exhibition, audio tapes, camera obscura.* April–October, Mon–Fri 11am–5pm, Sat 10am–5pm, Sun 2pm–5pm. November–March, Sat 10am–4.30pm, Sun 2pm–4.30pm.Small admission charge to non-residents. 0244 311610/321616.

King Charles' Tower, NE corner of city walls. *Displays on English Civil War.* April–October, Mon–Fri 1pm–5pm, Sat 10am–5pm, Sun 2pm–5.30pm. November–March, Sat 1pm–4.30pm, Sun 2pm–4.30pm. Small admission charge to non-residents. 0244 321616.

St Olave's, Lower Bridge Street. *Exhibition Centre in a converted church.* Mon–Sat 10.30am–5pm, Sun 2pm–5pm, closed between exhibitions. Admission free.

Gateway Theatre, *Telephone for details.* 0244 340392.

Northgate Arena Leisure Centre, *Swimming, dry sports, saunas, solaria, clubs, cafeteria.* 7 days. 0244 380444.

Chester Zoo, A41 (2 miles from city centre) *Animals, gardens, water bus, monorail, cafe, restaurant.* All year: 10am–dusk. Admission charge. 0244 380105.

Old Hall Conservation Centre, B1530 Aldford Road, Huntington. *Animals, video, craft shops, outdoor swimming (seasonal).* All year, Tue–Sun 10.30am–5.30pm. Free admission. 0244 350873.

Chirk, Clwyd

Chirk Castle, *A wealth of treasure from seven centuries, beautiful gardens.* End March–end September, daily not Mon & Sat 12pm–5pm October, Sat & Sun 12pm–5pm. Admission charge. 0691 777701.

Corwen, Clwyd

A small town on the A5 traditionally associated with Owain Glyndŵr, Corwen is situated towards the heart of North Wales. There is a walk to a monument on Pen-y-Pigyn above the town but the local landowner, Lord Newborough, denies all further access onto the mountain above, which has tremendous views. Locals go there anyway.

The Bunny Farm, A5104, 2 miles from the town. *Shetland Ponies, Pot-Bellied Pigs, Bunnies. Farm trail to hillfort.*March-end October, daily 10am–7pm. Admission charge. 0490 3180.

Ellesmere, Shropshire

Take plenty of wholemeal bread or muesli base for Ellesmere's main attraction, tame Canada geese and assorted species of ducks on The Mere.

The Meres Visitor Centre, *Displays and information on the meres, crafts.* Good Friday to end October daily and some weekends. Free admission. 0691 622981.

Ellesmere Port, Cheshire

Not to be confused with Ellesmere, the name comes from the wharfs at the junction of the Ellesmere Canal with the Mersey. Although this English town is some distance from the border, the canal museum is a must for anyone interested in the Llangollen Canal.

Boat Museum, (well signposted), *Canal boats, history, exhibitions and cafes.* April–October, daily 10am–5pm. November–March, not Friday 11am–4pm. Admission charge. 051 355 5017.

Holt, Clwyd *and Farndon*, Cheshire

Farndon (England) and Holt (Wales) are linked by an ancient bridge known respectively as Holt Bridge or Farndon Bridge depending on which country you favour. There is a picnic site on the English side of the river Dee and the remains of Holt Castle on the Welsh side. There are public paths on both sides of the river (the one south from Holt starts in the village). By crossing Holt Bridge and the bypass bridge south of the villages you can make an easy circular walk.

BOVIVM (Holt) was once the tile-works for the Roman 20th legion and the settlement was named on the Itinerary of Antonius as being 10 Roman miles from DEVA (Chester). Pieces of tile can still be found in the fields where the river path north of Holt meets an old lane.

Stretton Mill, off A534 Farndon–Broxton road. *Working water mill, demonstrations, displays.* Mar–end October, Tue–Sun & Bank Hol Mon 2pm–6pm. Small admission charge. 0606 41331.

Mold, Clwyd

A market town chosen as the site for the Clwyd County Council Civic Centre. The offices, county reference library and theatre stand ¾ of a mile above the town.

Theatr Clwyd (well signposted), *Theatre, cinema, exhibition centre and cafe.* 0352 755114.

Whitchurch, Shropshire

This small English town just a few miles across the border has plenty of places to stay and some interesting old buildings.

Whitchurch Swimming Pool, White Lion Car Park. 0948 4577.

Wrexham Maelor and the Clywedog Valley, Clwyd

There are four walks in the Clywedog Valley included in this book. For a longer walk follow The Clywedog Trail down the length of the valley. An official guide is available from Bersham Industrial Heritage Centre, Nant Mill and King's Mill.

For an extra long walk try The Maelor Way. This 24 mile waymarked country trail uses public footpaths, lanes and a canal towpath along the Welsh/English border. The Way links the Sandstone Trail, The South Cheshire Way, and The Shropshire Way with Offa's Dyke Path. It follows the rivers Dee and Ceiriog as well as meeting the Llangollen Canal at both ends. There is no need to walk the whole route in a day—the guide gives accommodation and other useful details (so you could walk only 8 miles for 3 days for example) and is available from most bookshops in the area.

Bersham Industrial Heritage Centre, Bersham.
The story of John 'Iron Mad' Wilkinson and the Davies brothers—gatesmiths, as well as regular exhibitions. Easter-end October, Tue–Sat & Bank Hols, 10am–12.30pm & 1.30pm–4pm, Sun 2pm–4pm. November–Easter, Tue–Fri, 10am–12.30pm & 1.30pm–4pm, Sat 12.30pm–3.30pm. Free admission. 0978 261529.

Nant Mill Visitor Centre, off Rhosberse Road, Coedpoeth. *Summer children's events, short nature trails, picnic area.* Easter–end September, Tue–Sun 10am–5pm. October–Easter, Sat & Sun 10am–4pm. Grounds open all year. Small admission charge to building. 0978 752772.

King's Mill, Kings Mill Road, off the A525, near Hightown. *The Miller's Tale, displays, video.* Easter–end September, Tue–Sun & Bank Hols 10am–5pm. October–Easter, Sat & Sun 10am–5pm. Grounds open all year. Small admission charge to building. 0978 362967.

Erddig near Wrexham (well-signposted). *National Trust House, gardens, country park.* April–end September, not Thur & Fri (except Good Fri) 11am–6pm. October, 11am–5pm (below stairs tour only), not Thur & Fri. Park open all year to walkers. House & garden admission charge to non-National Trust members. 0978 355314.

Ty Mawr Country Park, Cefn Mawr. *Riverside walks, childrens' events, animals, visitor centre.* Open daily all year. Free admission. 0978 822780. Welsh/English castle. Site open all year on a hill above the village.

Wrexham Maelor Heritage Centre, 47–49 King St. Wrexham (opp. Bus Station). *Wrexham history displays.* Mon–Sat 10am–5pm. Free admission. 0978 290048.

Shire Horse Centre, Alyn Waters Country Park, A483, Llay. *Demonstrations, antique waggons, rides, cafe.* Easter–end October, not Fri 10am–5pm. November–end February, Sat & Sun 10am–4pm. Admission charge. 0978 290972.

The Plassey Craft Centre, Eyton. *craft shops, cafe, nature trail, wildlife lake.* All year. 0978 780277.

Farmworld, off A483, rear of Erddig, Sontley. *Animals, farm trail, displays, shop, restaurant.* Admission charge. 0978 840697.

North Wales Autograss, *Cars racing on grass.* Occasional meetings. 0745 4016.

Swimming Baths, Holt Road, Wrexham. 0978 263795.

Plas Madoc Leisure Centre, Acrefair, Wrexham. *Tropical Lagoon, sports, cafe.* 0978 821600.

Wrexham Library & Arts Centre, Wrexham. *Regular art exhibitions, extensive library, childrens' music workshops, clubs and societies, cafe.* 0978 261932.

Grove Park Little Theatre, Wrexham. *Telephone for details.* 0978 351981.

Vale of Llangollen, Clwyd

If you enjoy the Llangollen walks in this book try the longer 'Walks in Clwyd' available from the tourist information office.

Plas Newydd, Llangollen. *Find out about the Ladies of Llangollen.* Easter–April & October, Mon–Sat 10am–5pm, Sun 10am–4pm. May–September, Mon–Sat 10am–7pm, Sun 10am–5pm. Grounds open all year. Admission charge to house. 0978 861514 (Curator).

ECTARC Llangollen. *European cultural exhibitons, bookshop, Arthurian Library.* Free admission. 0978 861514.

Llangollen Wharf. *Canal museum, mountain bikes, canoes, boat trips.* Daily Easter–October. 0978 860702.

Valle Crucis Abbey. *Cistercian Abbey ruin.* End Mar–end October, daily 9.30am–6pm. October–March, Mon–Sat 9.30am–4pm, Sun 2pm–4pm. Admission charge. 0978 860326.

Llangollen Station. *Steam trains, Christmas and Thomas the Tank Engine Specials.* Mainly summer season. 0978 860950, 0978 860951 (24 hours).

Motor Museum one mile from the town towards Horseshoe Pass. *British Automobilia.* Easter–October, daily 10am–5pm. Winter, Mon–Fri 10am–12.30pm, 1.30pm–5pm. Admission charge. 0978 860324.

Military Museum. *Artefacts from two world wars.* Open daily. Admission charge. 0978 861187.

MAPS & GUIDES

1:50 000 OS Landranger series

117 Chester Wrexham and surrounding area
126 Shrewsbury and surrounding area

1:25 000 Pathfinder series

773 Mold (Yr Wyddgrug) and Chester (West) SJ 26/36
790 Farndon, Holt and Tattenhall SJ 45/55
805 Corwen SJ 04/14
806 Llangollen and Wrexham (Wrecsam) South SJ 24/34
807 Whitchurch (Shropshire) and Malpas (Cheshire) SJ 44/54

827 Chirk (Y Waun) SJ 23/33
828 Ellesmere (East) and Prees SJ 43/53

Short walks

A set of 15 'Walks Around Wrexham Maelor' for sale in the Tourist Information Centre and Wrexham Reference Library gives circular routes complete with maps and written directions.
'Walks In Clwyd' cover much of the rest of Clwyd and some parts of Wrexham Maelor and are for sale in Bookland (Wrexham) and most Information Centres.
Two short walks from Nant Mill are available from the Visitor Centre there.

NORTH WALES WILDLIFE TRUST

Several sites in the area are owned or managed by the trust including:

Hafod Wood, Erddig
Sontley Moor, Erddig
Three-cornered Meadow (visits by arrangement only)
Marford Quarry
Pisgah Quarry, Froncysyllte

For membership or further details contact: North West Wildlife Trust, Welsh College of Horticulture, Northop, Mold, Clwyd CH7 6AA. 0352 86379.

COMPLAINTS ABOUT PUBLIC FOOTPATHS

Footpaths, bridges, signposts, crops, ferocious dogs, lone bulls etc on public paths in the border counties are dealt with by the councils listed below. The author would be grateful for a copy of all letters sent or, if you're unsure which authority to send it to, send two to me and I will pass one to the appropriate authority, and another to the Rambler's Association who try to ensure that work is carried out.

Wrexham Maelor Borough Council deal with their own problems:
Wrexham Maelor Borough Council,
Director of Public Works,
Rhostyllen House, Rhostyllen,
WREXHAM, Clwyd LL14 4DU.

otherwise all letters should be sent to the county councils:

Clwyd County Council,
Director of Highways and Transportation,
Shire Hall,
MOLD, Clwyd CH7 6NF.

Shropshire County Council,
Head of Countryside, Leisure Services Department,
Winston Churchill Building,
Radbrook Centre, Radbrook Road,
SHREWSBURY, Shropshire, SY3 9BJ.

Cheshire County Council,
County Heritage and Recreation Officer,
Public Rights of Way Department, Cheshire County Council,
Commerce House, Hunter Street,
CHESTER, Cheshire CH1 2QP.

WALKING GROUPS IN THE AREA

Rambler's Association, Wrexham Group.
Paul and Valerie Davies (Secretaries),
32 Peel Street,
WREXHAM, Clwyd LL13 7TR.
0978 362253

Whitchurch Walkers
Mrs O. M. Bishop (Secretary),
10 Richmond Terrace,
WHITCHURCH, Shropshire.
0948 2322

Wrexham Rambling Club,
David Roberts (Secretary),
0978 359140

Other walking clubs in Cheshire, Merseyside and Clwyd regularly use the Borderlands. For details of these send a SAE to:
The Ramblers
1/5 Wandsworth Road
London SW8 2XX
071-582 6878

Explore the villages, mountains, woods and waterways of Clwyd with these informative guides. Each booklet contains an interesting walk—shortcuts included—a map and line drawings of buildings, plants and animals. There are 26 booklets, available from bookshops, Tourist Information Offices and Clwyd libraries. Starting points are on Bus routes. Price 90p. Enquiries: 0244 377955.

FAMILY WALKS SERIES

Family Walks in the North Yorkshire Dales. Howard Beck. ISBN 0 907758 52 5.
Family Walks in West Yorkshire. Howard Beck. ISBN 0 907758 43 6.
Family Walks in Three Peaks and Malham. Howard Beck. ISBN 0 907758 42 8.
Family Walks in South Yorkshire. Norman Taylor. ISBN 0 907758 25 8.
Family Walks in the North Wales Borderlands. Gordon Emery. ISBN 0 907758 50 9.
Family Walks in Cheshire. Chris Buckland. ISBN 0 907758 29 0.
Family Walks in the Staffordshire Peak and Potteries. Les Lumsdon. ISBN 0 907758 34 7.
Family Walks in the White Peak. Norman Taylor. ISBN 0 907758 09 6.
Family Walks in the Dark Peak. Norman Taylor. ISBN 0 907758 16 9.
Family Walks in Snowdonia. Laurence Main. ISBN 0 907758 32 0.
Family Walks in Mid Wales. Laurence Main. ISBN 0 907758 27 4.
Family Walks in South Shropshire. Marian Newton. ISBN 0 907758 30 4.
Family Walks in the Teme Valley. Camilla Harrison. ISBN 0 907758 45 2.
Family Walks in Hereford and Worcester. Gordon Ottewell. ISBN 0 907758 20 7.
Family Walks around Cardiff and the Valleys. Gordon Hindess. ISBN 0 907758 54 1.
Family Walks in the Wye Valley. Heather and Jon Hurley. ISBN 0 907758 26 6.
Family Walks in Warwickshire. Geoff Allen. ISBN 0 907758 53 3.
Family Walks around Stratford and Banbury. Gordon Ottewell. ISBN 0 907758 49 5.
Family Walks in the Cotswolds. Gordon Ottewell. ISBN 0 907758 15 0.
Family Walks in South Gloucestershire. Gordon Ottewell. ISBN 0 907758 33 9.
Family Walks in Oxfordshire. Laurence Main. ISBN 0 907758 38 X.
Family Walks around Bristol, Bath and the Mendips. Nigel Vile. ISBN 0 907758 19 3.
Family Walks in Wiltshire. Nigel Vile. ISBN 0 907758 21 5.
Family Walks in Berkshire and North Hampshire. Kathy Sharp. ISBN 0 907758 37 1.
Family Walks on Exmoor and the Quantocks. John Caswell. ISBN 0 907758 46 0.
Family Walks in Mendip, Avalon and Sedgemoor. Nigel Vile. ISBN 0 907758 41 X.
Family Walks in Cornwall. John Caswell. ISBN 0 907758 55 X.
Family Walks on the Isle of Wight. Laurence Main. ISBN 0 907758 56 8.
Family Walks in North West Kent. Clive Cutter. ISBN 0 907758 36 3.
Family Walks in the Weald of Kent and Sussex. Clive and Sally Cutter. ISBN 0 907758 51 7.

The Publishers, D. J. Mitchell and E. G. Power welcome suggestions for further titles in this Series; and will be pleased to consider manuscripts relating to Derbyshire from new or established authors.
